A Primer on Legislative Support

A Primer on Legislative Support

Dr. Moitri Dey
Ms. Paromita Datta
Dr. Radha Kumari
Dr. Simer Preet Kaur

ADROIT
Adroit Publishers
NEW DELHI • KATHMANDU

ISBN : 978-81-87393-60-3

2018

Published by
ADROIT PUBLISHERS 4675/21, Ganpati Bhawan, Ansari Road,
Daryaganj, New Delhi-110 002 Phone : 011-23266030
adroitpublishers@gmail.com
C/O Vajra books, Thamel, Jyatha,
Kathmandu, Nepal l KTM: +977-9808357451

Typeset in Garamond Premier Pro by Arun, Akriti Graphic Solution, Delhi-110081 E-mail: arun263923@gmail.com, Ph: 9999414390

Contents

Preface ..... *vii*

Foreword ..... *xi*

Abbreviation ..... *xiii*

1. Parliamentary System In India 1
   Dr. Radha Kumari

2. Powers and Functions of People's Representatives 25
   Dr. Moitri Dey

3. Rural And Urban Local Self-Governance 41
   Dr. Simer Preet Kaur

4. Supporting the Legislative Process 69
   Ms. Paromita Datta

5. Committee System in India 93
   Dr. Radha Kumari

6. Budget and Budgetary Process in India 116
   Dr. Moitri Dey

7. Role of Media in a Democracy 138
   Dr. Simer Preet Kaur

8. Role of Civil Society Organisation in Legislative Process 151
   Ms. Paromita Datta

Annexure *169*

Index *176*

About the Authors *178*

Preface

The Choice Based Credit Course (CBCS) was introduced with an array of subject choices for the students. A new paper titled "Legislative Practices and Procedures" was introduced as Skill Enhancement Course for undergraduate Political Science honors students and a similar course titled : "Legislative Support" was introduced in B.A. Program as one of the electives for Skill Enhancement Course. Legislature plays a major role in the governing of the country. As a citizen of the country, the young minds should be aware, how the country is governed. This paper will enhance the knowledge of the students on the legislative process of the country. The purpose of the course is also to enhance the skills of the students and to broaden their understanding of the different tiers of governance in India. It endeavors to introduce the students with legislative procedures at various levels and also to introduce them to the roles and responsibilities of various stakeholders. Keeping the purpose of the course in mind, we have tried our best to bring out a concise text book for the same.

Within the framework of Governance, State occupies the most important place. So it is vital to know in any political system how the institutions work and respond to the demands of society in question. Ideally, a parliamentary form of government is looked at as a means to responsible and representative government. India became a republic in 1950 with the adoption of a parliamentary system by its constitution. The first chapter begins with the basic concept of governance and Parliamentary Democracy.

India is a federal state which derives its existence from the Constitution. One of the prominent features of the Indian federal structure is that there is division of powers between the federal government and the governments of the component states. The second chapter explains the power division and their functions. It elaborates on the powers and functions of Members of Parliament. It also explains the structure of State Legislative Assemblies. Further, it describes the powers and functions of Members of Legislative Assemblies.

In a large democratic country like India, central and state governments try to make good policies for all their citizens, but ensuring their implementation becomes a difficult task without the active participation of people at the grass root level. People's participation is one of the essential components of good governance in a democracy in particular. Active participation of people at all the levels ensures development and socio-economic growth at local as well as national levels. The chapter will help the students in understanding the structure and functioning of local governance which is the grassroots of democracy.

The Parliament is the supreme law-making body in the country. It plays an important role in guiding the society with progressive legislations. The amount of work done by Parliament is mammoth. With the ever-changing socio-economic conditions in the country the various functions and responsibilities of Parliament havealso increased to a large extent. This chapter will enable the students to understand the myriads of issues and challenges facing the society, new mechanisms have also been evolved within the legislative boundary which provide the Parliament with the requisite support to serve the people.

Since Parliament in India is a large body and plagued by many issue; like party politics, factionalism, etc. the actual work of Parliament is done through Parliamentary Committees. This chapter deals with the types, functions and restructuring of committee system in general and DRSCs in particular. Committee system of few other countries has also been incorporated to have a comparative perspective.

Budget is one of the most important components of governance. It is an essential activity carried out by government for performing governmental functions. This chapter explains the meaning and concept of Budget. It also elaborates the significance of Budget which is one of the important functions of the Parliament. The various types of Budgethave been described in the chapter. Further, it explains various types of funds in India. The chapter also elaborates the budgetary process in India which will help the students to understand the process of Budget formation in detail. Media has become an essential part of the present democratic traditions. It plays a significant role in preserving and upholding the democratic ethos and values in the society. It acts as a channel between the government and various stakeholders in the society. It provides the government with valuable information regarding the conditions prevailing at the ground level.So, the chapter will help the students in understanding theimportant role of media in the democracy of a country.

The chapter shows how Civil Society Organizations have become indispensable in today's world. Through their work, they influence and shape policies at both national and international level. They provide a platform for the common masses to present their views, opinions pertaining to matters of public importance. Thus, they also provide an opportunity to maintain public accountability of the Legislature towards the people. The inability of the Indian state to overcome the various challenges which arose due to the increasing demands of the society has encouraged and paved the way for the CSOs. The state no longer solely occupies the traditional space in the context of meeting the aspirations of the people.

Throughout the process of writing of this book many individuals haveextended their support to us. We take this opportunity to extend our gratitude to them. We would like to thank Shri S. Prem Singh Chandumajra, Member of Parliament, for giving us time from his tight schedule and writing a foreward for us. His words for the book are encouraging which will help us to take up such projects in future. We would also like to thank Shri S. Harinder Pal Singh, member DSGPC. Dr. Pradeep Sharma, Assistant Professor, Dept. of English, King Abdul Aziz University, Jeddah, Saudi Arabia; Dr. Ankita Verma, Consultant, National Development Skill Agency, Ministry of Skill Development, Government of India. Last but not the least, we would like to specially thank Mr. Akhil Sharma, Adriot Publishers, New Delhi for his swiftness in bringing out the book.

We would like to thank our students, the Department of Political Science and Mata Sundri College for Women for their encouragement.

Prem Singh Chandumajra
Member of Parliament
(Lok Sabha)

40, Pt Ravi Shankar Shukla
Lane (Canning Lane)
New Delhi-110001
Mobile: +91-9013869329

Foreword

Legislature formulates the will of the state into laws by giving it a legal character. It has the power to transform the demands of the people into authoritative laws/statutes. It is one of the most important works of any democratic state, and forms one of the three pillars on which democracy stands strong. Despite the nature and importance of the work clone by legislature, the general public for whom it works, has little or no knowledge about it.

Knowledge is a powerful factor that empowers people to achieve great results. The more knowledge a person gains, the more powerful they become. In a democracy, empowered and knowledgeable citizens can help in making our political system more responsive, accountable and citizen-friendly. Towards this goal, various acts have been passed by the parliament, like the Right to Information act of 2005, but more needs to be done to filter this right to the common citizen. Legislation is a difficult and significant work, and it's very important that the people, especially the youth of the country should not only know but understand it in its entirety. I was very glad to know that a paper on legislative practices has been introduced in all the central universities across the country under the Choice Based Credit System (CBCS) syllabus.

This book is a basic primer for anyone who wants to get an in-depth knowledge of how legislation works in India. This book provides a valuable window on various facets of our legislative processes and covers all the necessary components needed to understand it properly. The authors are working in the University of Delhi, and having taught it there, understand the course structure and requirements for such a topic. The book covers all the major works done by our Parliament and the authors seem to have done full justice to recognize, understand and impart full understanding of the subject.

I recommend this book as a must read for students, researchers, scholars and anyone else who wishes to understand the very important and indispensable role of our legislature and its supporting pillars.

Prem Singh Chandumajra
M.P. (L.S.)

PREM SINGH CHANDUMAJRA
MEMBER OF PARLIAMENT
LOK SABHA

ABBREVIATIONS

BDO	:	Block Development Officer
BJP	:	Bharatiya Janta Party
BPL	:	Below Poverty Line
CAARD	:	Committee on Administrative Arrangements For Rural Development And Poverty Alleviation
CAG	:	Comptroller And Auditor General of India
CAPART	:	Council for Advancement of People's Action and Rural Technology
CCS	:	Centre for Civil Society
CDP	:	Community Development Programme
CCPPRI	:	Concept Paper on Panchayati Raj Institutions
CSO	:	Civil Society Organisation
DRSC	:	Department Related Standing Committees
FCI	:	Food Corporation of India
GoI	:	Government of India
HC	:	High Court
MHRD	:	Ministry of Human Resourse Development
IMF	:	International Monetary Fund
IPC	:	Indian Penal Code
JNNURM	:	Jawaharlal Nehru National Urban Renewal Mission
JPC	:	Joint Parliamentary Committee
LPG	:	Liberalization, Privatization, and Globalization
LSTV	:	Lok Sabha Television

MCI	:	Medical Council of India
MLA	:	Member of Legislative Assembly
MP	:	Member of Parliament
MPLADS	:	Members of Parliament Local Area Development Scheme
MKSS	:	Mazdoor Kisan Shakti Sangathan
NCRWC	:	National Commission to Review the Working of the Constitution
NDA	:	National Democratic Alliance
NES	:	National Extension Service
NGOs	:	Non-Govermental Organisations
NITI Aayog	:	National Institution for Transforming India
OECD	:	Organization for Economic Cooperation and Development (OECD)
PAC	:	Public Accounts Committee
PESA	:	Panchayats (Extension to the Scheduled Areas Act)
PIL	:	Public Interest Litigation
PPB	:	Planning-Programming Budgeting
PRI	:	Panchayati Raj Institution
PUCL	:	People's Union for Civil Liberties
RSTV	:	Rajya Sabha Television
RTI	:	Right to Information
SAP	:	Structural Adjustment Programs
SC	:	Supreme Court
UNRISD	:	United Nations Research Institute For Social Development
UPA	:	United Progressive Alliance
USA	:	United States of America
UT	:	Union Territory
VSNL	:	Videsh Sanchar Nigam Limited

ONE

Parliamentary System In India

Dr. Radha Kumari

Since 1980's 'governance' has become a buzz word which refers to a complex set of institutions and actors. They have become part of the government and also beyond that. The term 'governance' has different meanings and can be used in a variety of ways. The term governance is closely linked with revision of the role of the state and its government institutions. This holds equally true about the legislative process in India. Still, within the framework of governance, State occupies the most important place. So, it is vital to know how the institutions work and respond to the demands of society in any political system. Constitution of any country lays down the rules for establishment of institutions and their relationships. Simultaneously, this is also true that other than government power, a network of other actors also affect the working of state and its institutions

Governance is an interactive process where government may like to impose its will but its acceptance depends on compliance and actions of others. In these relationships and networks, one institution cannot easily dominate. It will depend on a particular process of exchange. The monopoly of political institutions in providing services is diluted and the private sector and institutions of civil society fill in the space previously occupied by these institutions (Mathur, 2011). The term 'Governance' was first used by World Bank in 1989 regarding its report on Sub Saharan Africa, according to which this region was going through a 'crisis of governance.' The World Bank advocated for redefining the role of the state from government to governance. As it suggested a 'Slim' state having smaller size of bureaucracy with efficient infrastructure, privatization and liberalization became the new slogans of effective government. However, in this whole process the role of state was not reduced, rather reconceptualised. In fact, some developments in the world, particularly the recession of 2008-09, has emphasized the fact that liberal policies also need state's authority to direct and regulate the market to be successful. In fact, some of the scholars are of the view, particularly the 'realists,' that globalisation has further strengthened the role of state and its institutions. So, governance also means building capacities of government institutions and encouraging democratic participation. The concept of Governance recognizes the fact that things cannot be simply done by using power of government only. There has to be involvement of other actors as well, like civil society, media, market, and other political and non-political actors.

India gained its independence from British colonial rule in 1947 and adopted its constitution in 1950 which was democratic in its ethos as its preamble declares. India's transition to democracy was not well received by most of western scholars, sometimes ridiculed, and some of them even wrote its obituaries. This reaction, from a slew of scholars as well as politicians from the west, was not surprising as 'India of 1950' as a 'Political System', defies all those criteria considered necessary to be a successful democracy, namely – industrialisation, homogeneous society, 'civic culture,' wealth and so on. The following quote from a book clarifies the picture better.

"To abandon India to the rule of Brahmins (who in his opinion dominated the Congress Party) would be an art of cruel and wicked negligence. If the British left, he predicted then, the entire gamut of public services created by them – the judicial, medical, railway and public work departments - would perish, and India will fall back quite rapidly through the centuries into the barbarism and privations of the Middle ages" (Guha, 2012).

Now, after more than six decades there is little doubt that democracy in India, at least in procedural terms, has taken root. This success story of Indian democracy can be well understood by focusing on many factors -- like the way power entitlements have been bargained among the political elites of this country who are rivals, yet coalescent as well as interaction of state and society. The 'design' of Political institutions has also contributed to this success. The modern democratic institutions which India has adopted could be said to be of western origin and design. It however needs to be emphasized that our constitution framers tried to root them in Indian milieu, bringing them in conformity with the native realities. (Kohli, 2011).

Why Representative Democracy?

In 'The Republic' Plato argues that a boat must be directed by its captain. In Britain, there was a common saying that if a good despot could be ensured, despotic monarchy would be the best form of government. But J. S. Mill in his book 'Representative Government' has rejected the idea of despotic monarchy as being the good form of government, rather he looks upon this as a radical and the most pernicious misconception of good government. (Mill, 1865) Though, in India also the idea of 'enlightened monarchy' has been fascinating among common people in the form of a mythical concept of 'Ramrajya', yet by the time India became free from British Crown, monarchy was not an option for our constitution framers having even worth of being considered. This is also true that since the time of our freedom struggle, our political leaders were not in agreement regarding the political framework for India, as there were liberals, communists, Gandhians, socialists, and so on but one thing commonly held by them was that days of monarchy were over for India. This was the opinion of most of leaders from Congress and other political parties also of that time that if monarchy was not the right choice, so was the direct democracy except Gandhians.

In this connection, Neera Chandhoke writes that in eighteenth century France, the great defender of direct democracy, Jean-Jacques Rousseau, wrote that sovereignty lies essentially in the general will and the will does not admit of representation: it is either the same or the other; there is no intermediate possibility. She further adds, "But direct democracy can hardly be practised in large and complex societies. In market oriented societies, dominated as they are by the imperative of 'need satisfaction,' citizens cannot afford to put aside the time and energy- consuming task of earning their daily bread, and participate whole-time in an activity called politics. Besides, modern citizens, unlike ancient Athenians, value and guard their personal spaces, their vocation, their interests, their social life and their privacy. For these reasons and more, democracy requires a third set of political agents to mediate between the first two sets: the citizen and the state. This is the representative." (Chandhoke, 2016).

"It was Aristotle who argued that in a true republic while the laws must conform generally to popular will, yet at the same time the people must be ready to elect, for the conduct of state's affairs, men of superior training in public business whose guidance they will accept. If one wants a pair of shoes, one does not try to make them for oneself, but employs a cobbler, because of the latter's superior skill and experience and then reserves judgement for oneself as to whether the shoes fit or pinch. If shoes fit, one continues to employ the cobbler, otherwise another is sought." (Hall, 1921). Aristotle expressed these views at the time of Greek city states which seem to be more relevant in modern age. Professor Giddings, while recognising the shortcomings of indirect democracy gave a striking and statesmanlike summary of the relations of direct democracy to representative government in these words, "While no way has been found, or is likely to be found, to make a democracy fool proof, experience indicates that the best working system is a combination of direct democracy with representative government" (Giddings, 1921).

Definition of Parliamentary Democracy

Andrew Heywood has defined Parliamentary Democracy as, "A form of democratic rule that operates through a properly elected deliberative assembly, which mediates Government and the people. Democracy in this sense is responsible and representative Government. Parliamentary democracy thus balances popular participation against elite rule: Government is accountable not directly to the public but to the public's elected representatives. The alleged strength of such a system is that the representatives are, by virtue of their education and experience, better able than citizens themselves to define their best interests." (Heywood, 2013).

Besides representation, the Parliament is also a deliberative body which in fact underlies all the rest of the functions it performs, such as ventilating the grievances of the people, debating the major questions of the day, holding the Government accountable for its actions and expenditure, and exercising the constituent power of amendment. (Singh & Saxena, 2010). According to Neera Chandhoke, "Parliament makes laws, ensures accountability of the government, and considers and scrutinises legislation through committee system. But above all, Parliament provides a forum and establishes procedures for reflection on, and critical engagement with, what has been done and what needs to be done, in the light of popular expectations." (Chandhoke, 2016).

Evolution of Parliamentary System in India

The genesis of India's Parliament can be traced back to the British response to the crisis of 1857, in the form of 1858 Act, as the need for some form of consultancy and efficiency was already being felt by now. Though, the British didn't aim to establish a representative and accountable Government, yet growing pressure of English speaking Indian elite and the need of changing times, resulted in some form of deliberation and accountability. Thus, by the eve of World War one, Indians who were sitting in Legislatures, could debate budget and other issues now. (Hewitt & Rai, 2010).

The Act of 1935 laid an elaborate foundation of representative democracy and the federal system. The provisions of 1935 act influenced the constituent assembly in considering the parliamentary system favourably (Abbas, 2011). According to Subhash Kashyap, "The founding father preferred the parliamentary form because they had some experience of operating it and there were advantages in continuing established institutions. After a long struggle for responsible Government and against arbitrary executive authority, they were naturally allergic to a fixed term irremovable executive. In a highly pluralistic society with India's size and diversity and with many pulls of various kinds, they believed that the parliamentary form was most suited for accommodating a variety of interests and building a united India" (Kashyap, 2012).

While this decision was an outcome of our experience of Westminster Model, it would be erroneous to assume that British model was transplanted in India. Indian Parliamentary System has incorporated the provisions to best suit its own requirements. Though some other alternative models of legislative systems were also proposed and discussed in constituent assembly. As Mahatma Gandhi himself was never in favour of party system as well as of parliamentary democracy, philosophers influenced by Gandhian philosophy put an alternative model based on the village panchayat model. It was a model for direct democracy with an objective of having decentralisation of the highest level. However, there was no consensus on the Gandhian model. Nehru and Ambedkar were opposed to such a system, though for different reasons. Nehru had never reconciled with the vision of society proposed by Gandhi in his *Hind Swaraj*. Ambedkar expressed his apprehension of village panchayats becoming a means to perpetuate prevailing caste inequalities. As a result, parliamentary government model was adopted by the constituent Assembly. However, later on, the Gandhian Model also found its place in the Indian constitution, in the form of 73rd Constitution amendment act, 1992, through which, the village panchayats became the third tier of democracy in India (Abbas, 2011).

Indian Parliament

Article 79 of the Constitution maintains that there shall be a Parliament for the Union of India. Articles 79 to 123 have provisions regarding the composition, membership, conduct of business and powers of both the houses of Parliament. As already discussed, Indian Constitution has similar provisions of Parliamentary form of Government in its units too. Articles 168 to 213 of the Constitution deal with legislative structure in the states. In a Parliamentary structure, Executive is collectively responsible to the lower chamber of the Legislature.

The Indian Parliament represents the kind of democratic politics that few could have envisaged when universal suffrage was introduced in 1951. Its composition, especially in the Lok Sabha— the lower house or House of the People—has been a reliable index of the changing political preferences of Indian voters. The social composition of Parliament has changed considerably over the years, reflecting the general fluidity of power that has come to characterize Indian politics. India has become one of the more intensely politicized societies in the world, and many of these tensions are reflected in the debates and even in the chaos in Parliament. From its inception as an elite coterie of British educated lawyers, its members today are drawn from a variety of social strata and occupations. (Hewitt & Rai, 2010).

BI-Cameral Structure of the Parliament

The Parliament is bi-cameral in its structure. Reasons for having a bi-cameral structure in India were many; being a large and diverse country, second chamber is always seen a house representing different states. To have a provision of a permanent House in Parliament where the lower house, i.e. Lok Sabha can be dissolved anytime on advice of Council of ministers was another important reason in this regard. The need of a second thought to put brakes on the wheels of hasty decisions of Lok sabha was also one of the cited reasons during the debates of constituent assembly for having second chamber.

The President

Intimate relationship between Executive and Legislature is one of the underlying principles of Parliamentary system. In India, the President, the Chief Executive, has been made an integral part of Parliament. President's assent is mandatory for each bill to become a law whether it is a General Bill, Finance Bill or Constitutional Amendment Bill.

Rajya Sabha

Rajya Sabha or Council of States is the upper House of Parliament. This house cannot be dissolved, so it is permanent in nature. Indian Constitution puts a limit of maximum 250 members for Rajya Sabha, out of which President can nominate a maximum of 12 members from the people recognised as significant contributors from the fields of Art, Literature, Science and Social Services. Units in India have not been allotted equal seats in Rajya Sabha like in the Senate of USA. States get seats in Rajya Sabha in proportion to their population. Members are indirectly elected by state and union territories legislatures through single transferable vote system. Currently there are 245 members in Rajya Sabha.

One, most often cited logic for having second chamber, i.e., Rajya Sabha, is to have a house which could defend sub-national interests in a federal system. Though, the evidences of Rajya Sabha being successful to fulfil the objective, have been wanting. The reasons for this are many:

- For any joint sitting, which is a rare case, Lok Sabha has numerical superiority over Rajya Sabha

- With regard to money bill, Rajya Sabha is the weakest house among upper chambers of the world.
- Dominance of Congress party for a long period in the past also rendered Rajya Sabha just as a cheering House for Lok Sabha.

Changing Trends in Rajya Sabha

In recent years, however, broader political trends have increased the importance of the Rajya Sabha, although it is still limited, if compared with the Lok Sabha. First, the rise of regional parties, which began to control state governments more pervasively, has resulted in a greater divergence in the party affiliations of Rajya Sabha and Lok Sabha members. The different electoral cycles of the two houses, coupled with the absence of a dominant party have meant that a party or coalition with a majority in the lower house is not guaranteed the same in the upper house. This has meant that the ruling coalition can be in a minority in the Rajya Sabha, which gives the upper house effective veto power on non-budget bills; although in rare cases the government can call a joint session of Parliament. This has meant that the government in power needs cooperation of the opposition to get bills passed and has also made it increasingly difficult for parties to muster the two-third majority needed to amend the Constitution. (Kapur & Mehta, 2006).

There are many recent examples when government of the day could not make laws of its own choice. Failed efforts of the NDA government for amending Land Acquisition Amendment Bill passed by its predecessor the UPA government is one important example in this regard. Though it has also led to other fallouts in the form of growing trends of promulgation of ordinances which would be discussed later in detail.

Keeping in view the obstacles in legislation and to have a uniform mandate in both the houses, Bhartiya Janta Party is advocating simultaneous elections of Lok Sabha and Vidhan Sabhas as one major electoral reform after its clear majority in the 16th Lok Sabha. One of the prominent leaders from BJP has also raised the point of amending the constitution for provision of reservation for women in the Parliament only if the party manages to get required numbers in Rajya Sabha too. Though this is a matter of investigation that which one is the main obstacle for the provision of reservation for women in Parliament; political will or this institutional mechanism? Yet this is again an example to prove that in a genuine multi-party system of now in India, Rajya Sabha is no more a toothless house.

Lok Sabha

Lok sabha is the lower house of Indian Parliament to which Council of Ministers is collectively responsible. Being a directly elected House, it exercises more powers in comparison to Rajya Sabha; particularly in financial matters. Indian Constitution has put a limit of maximum 552 members in Lok Sabha out of which a maximum of 530 can be elected from states on the 'the first past the post' basis, 20 from Union Territories and 2 members can be nominated form Anglo-Indian community by the President, if in his opinion the community has not got adequate representation in Lok Sabha. Currently the strength of Lok Sabha, including the nominated seats, is 545. This house has a tenure of five years but can be dissolved by the President at any time on the advice of Council of Ministers.

Changing Trends in Lok Sabha

In Lok Sabha, number of Members having better levels of education is growing for last two decades. But the paradox here is that despite a good number of members having higher education, Parliament is less competent for legislative work. Another trend is of growing number of new entrants in Lok Sabha which on the one hand is good, being an indicator of lot of youth energy willing to contribute to politics directly, but on the other hand, this results in lesser number of experienced members which is equally vital for legislation. (Kapur & Mehta, 2006).

The Executive

India has adopted the Westminster model of parliamentary democracy, with provisions of dual executives. Head of the state is called nominal executive, whereas head of the government is called the real executive. Unlike Great Britain, India is a republic, so the nominal executive, i.e., the President is not a monarch, assuming his/her position on the basis of heredity but an elected body. The Real Executive is known as Prime

Minister who heads the Council of Ministers. In a Parliamentary system, Legislature and Executive are closely linked to each other. In fact, all executive members have to be members of legislature. In case any member who is sworn-in as minister but is not a member of Parliament at the time, has to become member of the parliament within a period of six months. Prime-Minister and its Council of Ministers are collectively responsible to the lower House of Parliament, i.e. Lok Sabha. Though the real Executive has a term of 5 years, it does not enjoy a fixed term because Lok Sabha may pass a motion of no-confidence to topple the Government before the completion of its tenure. These provisions were adopted to ensure better co-ordination between executive and legislature as well as constant accountability of the Government towards legislature. How far these objectives have been achieved, needs a deeper analysis.

The Judiciary

Independent Judiciary is the first and foremost need of a democracy. In independent India judiciary has been made independent of Executive and technically it is not part of the legislative structure also; yet judiciary has the final say on laws made by the Parliament as it possesses the power to review the constitutionality of any law and constitutional amendment made by the Parliament. In the history of independent India there has been a period of competition for this final say between judiciary and Parliament. The concept, 'Basic Structure of the Constitution' invented by Judiciary itself in India, has ultimately made Judiciary the final authority in this regard.

Though India has federal structure of Government but in judicial arena it is integrated hierarchy based system where Supreme Court of India is the Highest Court of appeal which can accept appeals against the high Courts of its states. Since the last decade of twentieth century judicial activism has been a buzz word in India as Judiciary has been pro-actively taking the lead in work, which should be done by Legislature and Executive. This pro- activism of judiciary is now a debatable issue among scholars as some of them find it an encroachment over the jurisprudence of legislature, as well as the deviation from democratic norms.

Parliamentary Democracy with Federal Provisions

According to M.P.Singh, "Federalism along with parliamentarianism is another axial principle of government of India. These two principles are contradictory in the sense that parliamentary government is premised on legislative supremacy while federalism is predicated on decentralisation of political power." (Singh & Saxena, 2010). Indian Constituent assembly chose system of Parliamentary Democracy with federal provisions because of the vast size of India and the belief that this combination could best reflect the aspirations of our people. As many critics find India a relatively centralised state, this observation does not deny the fact that division of powers as well as accountability are the values which have been sought after most with such an institutional design. Representative parliamentary democracy constitutes the fundamentals of Indian Political System in which Legislature occupies the most important place. Since India is a federal system, the Indian Parliament also represents its constituent states, via the second chamber, the Rajya Sabha. All 29 states of India also have parliamentary structure of government, similar to that of the centre There are seven union territories which are directly governed by appointees of the centre, two of them, namely- Delhi and Puducherry, have their own elected legislatures.

Union-State Relations

Legislative Relations

Federalism shapes all kind of relationships between centre and its units, like- legislative, administrative, fiscal and financial. This chapter deals only with legislative relations as this is the main subject of concern here. The powers between centre and states have been assigned by seventh schedule of our constitution in three lists, namely, Union, State and Concurrent. In the words of M.P.Singh and Rekha Saxena, "......the division is based on the principles of subsidiarity and concurrency. By subsidiarity, it is meant that whichever level of Government can handle a particular subject more effectively is granted that subject. By concurrency, it is meant that the subjects in the twilight zone are allocated to both orders of Government with the laws made by the Parliament prevailing over those made by state legislatures in cases of conflicts." (Singh & Saxena, 2010).

The Union list is the longest list having 97 subjects to its credit. State list has 66 subjects and the concurrent list has 47 items on it. Though there have been some amendments, resulting in some omissions and additions in the lists, yet the number of items remains the same. In effect state list has lost some items, whereas other two lists have gained some. The largest of all the amendments regarding the division of powers has been forty second amendment. Other than these three lists, residual powers have been assigned to centre by default. So it can be easily concluded here that division of power is tilted in favour of centre.

There are many other articles too which give the Parliament an upper hand over state legislatures regarding their role in legislation. Article 249, 252 and 253 of the constitution are worth mentioning here, which, under certain circumstances authorize the Parliament to enact laws for State legislatures. Under article 249, Rajya Sabha can pass a resolution to make laws on a subject in State list, by two-third majority of its present and voting members if it deems it to be necessary in the interest of the nation. At times two or more than two State legislatures may also request (under article 252) Parliament to make laws for them, though such laws would be applicable only for those requesting states only. Again, Parliament, under article 253, has the authority to make any law for whole or any part of the country to bring in effect any international treaty, agreement, convention or decision. This is the legal institutional aspect of power sharing in Indian state, but this is also important to note here that the federal structure is also shaped by the political realities of the country where the different permutations and combinations of many factors like, political leadership, strength of national parties and regional parties, etc. play a major role.

Structure of Government in States

As discussed above, units of Indian union also have parliamentary form of government in which Governor is the nominal Executive and the Chief Minister is the real Executive.

Governor, as the Chief Executive in states is the integral part of State legislature. Bihar, Maharashtra, Andhra Pradesh, Telangana, Karnataka, Uttar Pradesh and Jammu-Kashmir have provision of bicameral legislature. All other states have single house in their Legislatures. Establishment or abolishment of a second chamber can be done on the request of state legislative assembly to the Parliament.

Vidhan Parishad

The upper house of the state legislature is called Vidhan parishad. Vidhan Parishad is a permanent Chamber which cannot be dissolved. Members of Vidhan Parishad enjoy a term of 6 years. One third of its total members retire on completion of two years. However, the size of Vidhan Parishad cannot be less than 40 members (except in Jammu and Kashmir, where the Parliament has decided its membership to be maximum 36).

Vidhan Sabha

The lower house of state legislature is called Vidhan Sabha .This is a directly elected house of which membership has been decided maximum up to 500 and a minimum of 60. However, states like Sikkim, Goa, Mizoram and Union Territory of Puducherry can have smaller size of their Vidhan Sabhas by an act of Parliament, made keeping in view the smaller size of population in these states. Council of Ministers in States is collectively responsible to this house. This house has tenure of 5 years, if not dissolved early.

Panchayati Raj Institutions

Narsimha Rao led congress Government introduced 73rd and 74th amendments to the Constitution in 1992 which were enacted in 1993. These amendments were intended to create a third tier of governance in India for which 11th and 12th schedules were added to the constitution. The principal objective behind the amendments was that these institutions would be able to act autonomously within the domain delegated to them by state laws. But the objective was not achieved in its true spirit as these powers of PRIs have been made dependant on the discretion of the respective state governments. So, it is not the further division of power, rather it is devolution of power which was left on the discretion of the respective state legislatures. In fact this list of 29 subjects is only suggestive and studies are there to tell that across the country there is no significant change in the functional domains of Gram Panchayats.

However, the Constitutional Amendment Act has made significant advances over the past decades. It made it mandatory that elections be held every five years and will be conducted by State Election Commission. A uniform three tier structure was envisaged with Gram Sabha or the village assembly as the deliberate body of decentralised governance and the foundation of the Panchayat system. Women empowerment was mandated by reserving one-third seats in all the elected bodies as well as among the office of chairpersons in each tier. Reservations for scheduled castes and tribes were also provided. To ensure adequate financial resources to the Panchayats, the act has envisaged setting up of a state finance commission every five years. District planning Committees were made mandatory and given constitutional status. (Mathur, 2011).

Functions of Legislature in India and their Assessment

Traditionally, law–making is the supreme job of a legislature. According to Andrew Heywood, "To classify assemblies simply as legislature, debating chambers or representative bodies obscures their true significance." (Heywood, 2013). Though the functions vary from state to state and system to system, yet there are some functions which are identified with the legislature in general. Indian Parliament is the apex institution for legislation in India. Though Indian Constitution has provisions of division of power, yet it cannot be denied that this division of powers is tilted in favour of Parliament. Other than legislation for centre, for states and Union territories in special circumstances, our Parliament performs a fair number of functions. Subhash Kashyap has termed Indian Parliament 'A Multi-Functional Institution,' which performs variety of roles, which are inter-related. Some of the main functions performed by the Indian Parliament in his opinion are:

- To form or end the government
- To represent the electorate
- To legislate
- To hold the government accountable for its functions
- To monitor the expenditure of public funds
- To be a forum for debate

- To be a forum for the expression of grievances
- To call for information (Kashyap, 2012)

The supposed functions of Indian Parliament, in the words of Neera Chandhoke, can be summarised as follows: "Parliament makes laws, ensures accountability of the government, and considers and scrutinises legislation through committee system. But above all, Parliament provides a forum and establishes procedures for reflection on and critical engagement with, what has been done and what needs to be done, in the light of popular expectations." (Chandhoke, 2016).

While fully conceding to views given by scholars cited above, I would like to add a different angle of the whole legislative process. If one keeps aside legal and institutional approach for a while for the purpose of fully appreciating the issues, one would find that some of the functions apparently performed by the Parliament are actually intervened and further impacted by many surrounding factors. In the following paragraphs each function performed by the Parliament in procedural terms, have been assessed with the practical aspect of the same.

1. **Enacting Laws**

   The Indian Constitution has provisions of division of legislative powers in three lists, namely, the Union List, the State List and the Concurrent List in the seventh schedule. The parliament has exclusive jurisdiction over the matters included in Union List, whereas the subjects included in Concurrent list are under the concurrent jurisdiction of the Parliament and State legislatures both. However, in case of any conflict between the laws enacted by the Parliament and state legislature, the law of former will prevail. Though, State legislatures have jurisdiction over the matters in State List, yet under Article 249, the Parliament may legislate on matters of state List, if the Rajya Sabha declares any issue of national interest under the same Article. In case of emergency proclamation or President's rule respectively, under Article 352 or 356, Parliament gets the authority to enact laws on matters of State List. Amendment in Indian constitution is also a prerogative of our Parliament. Except for a few matters, for which nod of more than half of the state assemblies is required; Parliament is the only institution which is authorised to amend the Constitution under Article 368.

However, law making is not just a legal procedure. A lot of politics is always involved in as this activity takes place in a political environment. There are rules for legislation which have been amended many times to suit the need of the time. These rules can be and have been used by the establishment as well as opposition for political gains. Under these rules only a bill passed by both the Houses and consented to by the President, cannot be enforced until it is notified in the gazette. A good example of such play of politics is: A law on 'Benami' property passed in 1988 during Rajiv Gandhi's government lay dormant as it was neither notified in gazette nor its rules were framed. While conceding to the impact of political factors on law making procedure, it is equally important to assess the effects of other factors on the legislation process in India. For example, our representatives are generally more concerned with the prospects of getting re-elected. This re-election is less to do with their legislative skills than to work for the party organisation because in India, voting is done more for parties than for individual candidates so the job of legislation becomes secondary for them.

2. Representation

'No taxation without representation', is a very popular slogan of American Revolution that took place in 18th century. Now in 21st century, even monarchs also need legitimacy for exercising authority. India is a representative democracy which is based on universal suffrage. The members of Parliament are elected representatives of people and they are supposed to work as a link between Government and the people. Now a days when sessions of Parliament are directly telecast, this function has assumed greater prevalence in relation to others. All Members of Parliament want to be seen as a real guardian of their constituency's interests.

But, there is something more than meets the eye. Representation is a complex principle, and Burkean idea of representatives (as independent actors, 'trustee' using their own wisdom) as well as Thomas Paine's idea of a 'Delegate' (acting as a conduit of its electorates), do not apply to Indian Parliamentarians. Being a parliamentary system, particularly doctrine of mandate in which political parties occupy the main place and dictate all the decisions of representatives, seems to be more functional here. Members hardly seem to be crossing their party lines irrespective of the interests of the people they claim to represent. One more thing would be interesting and important to add here that these members often claiming to represent their constituency make the Parliament a site for grandstanding, leaving the substantial matters aside. Anti-defection law of 1985 also has made it impossible for members of legislative bodies to represent the interests of their constituencies in a non-partisan manner.

3. **Governmental Accountability (Political and Financial)**

In democracy, people are sovereign in principle. The Executive, which is responsible for administration of all kinds of work, is thus made accountable to representatives of people in indirect democracy. In Parliamentary democracy, this accountability of Executive to Legislature is very significant. On the same pattern, in India, our council of Ministers does not enjoy a fixed term; rather it is continuously liable to prove its confidence in lower house of Parliament. Other than that, Executive has been made accountable in many more ways. In any house of Parliament, government has to answer the questions of members of parliament. These members can criticise government, draw attention to any matter which they deem important.

Finance is the most important aspect of administration. Parliament has power to levy or modify taxes. No taxes can be legally levied, and no expenditure can be done without parliamentary authorization. The Lok Sabha, being a directly elected house, exercises more powers than Rajya Sabha in this regard. Committees like, Estimate Committee, Public Accounts Committee and Committee on Undertakings play a very important role regarding exercising oversight on the Executive in financial matters.

Yet, the important point to note here is that political accountability of government is most suppressed by the frequent promulgation of ordinances which was supposed to be used only in case of emergent need. In practice, however, instead of an exceptional measure, ordinance route is being taken by central and state governments both on a regular basis just to by-pass the legislature. Article 123 provides that any ordinance shall have same effect and force as any statute of Parliament, provided it is laid before both the houses within six week's period in the subsequent session. But to avoid deliberation and argument, these governments repromulgate the same ordinance again and again. Having force and effect of a statute, these ordinances may create such outcomes which are irreversible. A judgement given on 2nd January 2017 by the Supreme Court in Krishna Kumar Singh vs. State of Bihar can be expected to have positive outcomes for the future of democratic governance which clearly condemns this practice and instructs governments to avoid the same in future.

As far as financial accountability is concerned, so many lacunas exist there. Indian Constitution does not allow Executive to levy or collect any tax without the approval of Parliament. Our constitution has established consolidated fund wherein all the money collected from taxes is deposited. Government needs a prior approval from the legislature to withdraw money for expenditure. There is yet another fund called 'contingency fund' for emergent situations like, natural calamity, etc., viewing the need of expedited procedure of drawing funds in such situations, Executive has been exempted from the need of prior approval. In practice, transfer of money keeps going on from contingency fund to consolidated fund without an approval. Even parliament itself has not insisted on the need of such approval in many cases, consequently abdicating its responsibility. (Kapur & Mehta, 2006).

After liberalization, this accountability of government has further decreased as parliament has not taken active role in monitoring the executive as far as international treaties are concerned. One often cited counter argument here is the compulsion of incorporation into domestic legislation of such treaties to be effective. Even then the practice in Indian politics shows that treaty once signed is seen as a fate accompli. Now when the impact of international treaties is as pervasive as any act passed by the Parliament, these gaps in accountability are of major concern.

However, this is also important to note that control of Legislature over Executive in parliamentary system may prove to be a mere fiction when Executive has a clear majority in lower house. India has been no exception in this regard.

4. **Executive Functions of Parliament**

Our parliament functions as an electorate body also. Elected members of Parliament and Legislative Assemblies in states and union territories vote for the election of the President of India. Members of Parliament vote to elect the Vice-President as well. Article 61 gives judicial powers also to the Parliament, as any proposal of impeachment can be brought and decided over through a due process by the members of Parliament only. Removal of Supreme Court judges, CAG and Chief Election Officer can also be done by Parliament through the prescribed procedure in the Constitution

However, election of President is a prerogative of the elected members of legislative bodies, yet the party discipline has a vital role to play here. Right from the selection of the candidates for the post till voting, every act is decided at party meetings. The same happens with the other recruitments.

5. **Political Training and Informative Functions**

In this age of democracy, this function becomes far more important. Parliament is a forum for debate, discussions, deliberations and expression of people's expectations as well as grievances. Through direct telecast, laymen also get to know about the way Parliament works. There are special sessions for questions through people who also get vital information about their system. Such information and informal political training is vital for a country aspirant of having a sound political culture. Not just people, rather, the parliamentarians themselves go through formal induction and training sessions in Parliament. Parliament organises training sessions for people from academia also to give them the first-hand experience of parliamentary procedures and practices.

Though this is an informal function of the Parliament, which can be rather said to be a by-product of legislative process, the main actors behind the scene are political parties. The issues taken up in parliamentary meetings and the stand of members of parliament are approved much before by the party 'high command.'

Strength and Weakness of Indian Parliamentary System

Ideally, a parliamentary form of government means responsible and representative government. The primary function of the Legislature is to act like a national Congress of the people by proper representation and to ensure that the responsibility and accountability of the Executive to the Legislature is impeccably maintained. Heywood has noted that generally, 'during the twentieth century, the power and status of assemblies have changed for the worse.' This understanding emanates from the perspective of looking at assemblies as providing or failing to provide a responsible and accountable Government and as a deliberative body. He identifies four factors that could have contributed to the same, in general, in all parliamentary governments. We can apply them to see how they relate to the Indian situation:

- The emergence of disciplined political parties.
- The growth of 'big government.'
- The organisational weakness of assemblies.
- The rise of interest groups and media power (Heywood, 2013).

As has already been discussed that Indian parliamentarians work neither on the Burkean notion, as trustees of people, nor as delegates of their electorates (consulting everything with the people from their constituency), as suggested by French scholar, Thomas Paine. As a result, political parties are highly disciplined and organised here which have a culture of 'High Command' for central leadership. Parties have provision of whip, by which, any decision made by members of Parliament in house is pre-decided. With the introduction of Anti-defection law of 1985, this whip culture has become more strengthened. India is a multi-party democracy. Last two decades have witnessed coalition governments in centre as well as in many states also. These coalition governments were big in size due to tug of war among coalition partners to have more and important ministries under their control. This tendency has also led to the lack of principled politics and opportunist alliances. In absence of such commitment to principles, the level of debate is bound to decline.

Moreover, understanding legislation in terms of institutions and procedures only does not present the real picture. A lot of politics is involved in the whole process of a bill becoming an Act. So, legislative process cannot be understood fully without incorporating all the actors involved at various levels. Civil society organisations, media, interest groups, and pressure groups do play their roles in influencing the whole process of legislation. Law making and media have been closely linked since the advent of the press. With the revolutionary advancement in the realm of communication, this link has got strengthened. Now-a-days 'media trial' is the common popular word which actually indicates the extent of influence media has on the functionality of government. Parliament is an institution which reflects people's grievances. Now various interest groups and civil society organisations immediately take up such issues. With the growing commercialisation, a race for breaking news (covered rightly or wrongly) attracts people more than assembly debates.

In this age of information and technology, issues are getting more complex day by day. Our parliamentarians, having been elected on the basis of popularity, are not equipped with expertise required for administration. Though, DRSCS and other committees have provided a solution to this problem, yet this weakness of our Parliament has added to its declining credibility. India has one more feature, that is, of 'washed-up' sessions. The Winter Session of December 2016 was kept on hold on the single issue of demonetisation, and this was not the exception. Most of the business to be transacted through Parliament is either gets postponed or done through ordinance route, which is not a healthy trend for a democracy.

Lack of Non-Governmental Inputs and Informed Debate

Public policy is often is made without adequate input from outside government and without adequate debate on the issues involved. The best expertise in many sectors lies outside the Government. Yet the policy processes and structures of Government have no systematic means for obtaining outside inputs, for involving those affected by policies or for debating alternatives and their impacts on different groups. Most developed countries have a system of widespread public debate before a policy is approved. For example, in the US, the legislature subjects a new policy initiative to extensive debate not only in committees but also in the Senate and the House. Such debates not only enable an assessment of different viewpoints but also help build up a constituency in support of the policy through sound arguments. Probably, the only example of fairly systematic consultation of outside expertise in India is in the process of formulating the Central Budget, where there is a long tradition of pre-budget confabulations with chosen members of industry, labour and the academia.

Conclusion

In the words of Neera Chandhoke, "Democratic governance is complex, time consuming and demanding. Each proposal has to go through several stages for scrutiny, including debates in the public sphere on the virtues, or otherwise, of the proposition on offer, before it is transformed into law. The insertions layers of intermediary institutions that range from elected assemblies to civil society organisations, between citizens and the state, safeguards ordinary citizens against abuses of power," (Chandhoke, 2016).

Indians had great hopes that universal suffrage would produce a quiet and steady social revolution that would loosen the power structure of Indian society, ensure to all Indians the expansive list of rights promised to them under the constitution and bring about greater well-being. India's overall record in this matter is decidedly mixed. While it has sustained free institutions, widened the scope of democratic participation compared to its own historical past and made significant gains in economic growth—especially in recent years—India's performance on a range of human development and governance indicators is still decidedly lacklustre. (Kapur & Mehta, 2006).

After a scrutiny of performance of legislature, it becomes clear that there is an urgent need of reforms to maintain trust of people in this institution. Actually, it is Legislature only which provides foundation for the executive to work upon in forms of laws of the land. Even a cursory glance at the whole development of parliamentary procedures and practices is enough to show that there have been sincere efforts in this direction. While conceding to this claim, need for further reforms also cannot be ruled out. Yet, it is equally important to keep in mind that the legislature does not work in a vacuum; to improve the whole process of legislation there is equal need to work on those political factors and institutions which are often at the root of the problem.

Review Questions:

1. Discuss the evolution and structure of parliamentary system in India. Also, critically examine its strength and weakness.
2. Discuss the merits and demerits of a bi-cameral legislature with special reference to Indian context.
3. "Legislative process operates in a political context" What is your opinion regarding this observation? Give reasons in support of your response in either case.
4. Discuss the functions of Indian parliament in detail.
5. Write short notes on:
   a) Changing role of Rajya Sabha,
   b) Need of representative democracy in present times,
   c) Parliamentary democracy.

References:

1. Abbas, H., Kumar, R., & Alam, M. A. (2011). "Indian Government and Politics". New Delhi: Longman & Pearson, India.
2. Chandhoke, N. (2016). "The Unmaking of Parliament."The Hindu, 19 December 2016.
3. Giddings, F. H. (1921). 'Understanding our Government.' In Hall, A. B. (1921), Popular Government: An Inquiry into the Nature and Methods of Representative Government. New York: The Macmillan Company.
4. Guha, R. C., (2012). "India After Gandhi: The History of World's Largest Democracy". New Delhi: Picador India (an imprint of Pan Macmillan Ltd.).

5. Hall, A. B. (1921). "Popular Government: An Inquiry into the Nature and Methods of Representative Government." New York: The Macmillan Company.
6. Heywood, A. (2013). "Politics." New Delhi: Palgrave Macmillan India.
7. Hewitt, V., & Rai, S. M. (2010). 'Parliament.' In Mehta, P.B., & Jayal, N.G. (ed.), "The Oxford Companion to Politics in India," New Delhi: Oxford University Press.
8. Kapur, D., & Mehta, P. B. (2006). "The Indian Parliament as an Institution of Accountability." In Democracy, Governance and Human Rights, Paper Number 23, United Nations Research Institute for Development. Available at: http://www.unrisd.org/UNRISD/website/document.nsf, accessed on 14.7.2017.
9. Kashyap, S. (2012). "Our Parliament." New Delhi: National Book Trust, India.
10. Kohli, A. (2011). :"The Success of India's Democracy". edited by Atul Kohli. New Delhi: Cambridge University Press.
11. Mathur, K., (2011). "From Government to Governance: A Brief Survey of Indian Experience". New Delhi: National Book Trust of India.
12. Mill, J. S. (1865). "Considerations on Representative Government". London: Longman, Green, Longman, Roberts, and Green.
13. Singh, M. P., & Saxena, R. (2010). "Indian Politics: Contemporary Issues and Concerns." New Delhi: Prentice Hall India.

TWO

Powers and Functions of People's Representatives

Dr. Moitri Dey

India is a federal state which derives its existence from the Constitution. One of the prominent features of the Indian federal structure is that there is division of powers between the federal government and the governments of the component states. Article 1 of the Constitution declares that India, that is Bharat, shall be a Union of States. Part XI of the Indian Constitution defines the power distribution between the federal government (the Centre or the Union) and the States in India. This part is divided between legislative, administrative and executive powers. The legislative power is further divided into three lists i.e. Union list, State list and Concurrent list.

The Seventh Schedule, Article 246 of the Indian Constitution has listed out the Union list where Parliament has exclusive power to make laws with respect to any of the matters enumerated in List I in the Seventh Schedule referred to as the Union List. Similarly, the Legislature of the State has exclusive power to make laws with respect to any of the matters enumerated in List II known as the State List. The Union Parliament as well as the State Legislatures has the power to legislate over the subjects listed in List III in the Seventh Schedule referred to as the Concurrent List.

Article 248 states "The Union Parliament has exclusive power to make any law with respect to any matter not enumerated in the Concurrent List or the State List. Such power shall include the power of making any law and imposing a tax not mentioned in either of these lists". Thus, the Constitution of India creates a clear-cut division of legislative powers between the Union and the States. However, the Parliament holds a place of dominance and supremacy in the structure of governance. The Parliament is the highest law making body of the country and also it is the highest representative institution of the people (Kashyap, 2008). Members of Parliament are the representatives of the people. So, they are given certain power to carry out the functions of the Parliament.

Eligibility of a Member of Parliament

The Indian Parliament consists of the President, the Lok Sabha (House of the People) and the Rajya Sabha (Council of States). The President is the head of the state and is elected by an Electoral College. The Electoral College consists of the elected members of the two Houses of the Parliament and Legislative Assemblies of the States. The Lok Sabha has 530 members representing the states, 20 members representing the Union Territories and 2 members to be nominated by the by the President from the Anglo-Indian Community. At present, there are 545 members. The Lok Sabha members are directly elected by the citizens of India who are eligible to vote. Voting rights in India are given at the age of 18 to the citizens unless he/she is disqualified under law (Article 326). The Lok Sabha dissolves after every five years.

The Rajya Sabha consists of 250 members which includes 238 members representing the States and Union Territories. The members of the Rajya Sabha are elected by the elected members of the State Legislative Assemblies. The President nominates two members of Anglo-Indian community in Lok Sabha and twelve members who have excelled in various fields such as art, literature, science, social service, etc. in the Rajya Sabha. Rajya Sabha is a permanent body; one-third members retire every second year and are replaced by newly elected members. Each member is elected for a term for six years.

According to Article 84 of the Constitution of India, qualifications of a person for membership of Parliament are:

1. He/She is a citizen of India, and makes and subscribes before some person authorized in that behalf by the Election Commission an oath or affirmation according to the form set out for the purpose in the Third Schedule.
2. He/She has completed 30 years of age in case of Rajya Sabha and 25 years of age in case of Lok Sabha.

3. He/She possesses such other qualifications as may be prescribed on that behalf by any law made by Parliament.

Apart from the above conditions, the Parliament included other qualifications of Member of Parliament in the Representation of People Act, 1951 (GoI, 1951). Part 2 of the Act states various other qualifications for membership of Parliament. These qualifications are:

1. To be qualified as member of the Rajya Sabha, he/she must be registered as a voter in a parliamentary constituency and must be eligible to vote. In case a person loses credibility to vote, he/she lose eligibility to vote.

Qualifications for membership of the Lok Sabha – A person shall not be qualified to be chosen to fill a seat in the Lok Sabha unless –

a. in the case of a seat reserved for the Scheduled Castes in any State, he is a member of any of the Scheduled Castes, whether of that State or of any other State, and is an elector for any Parliamentary constituency;
b. in the case of a seat reserved for the Scheduled Tribes in any State (other than those in the autonomous districts of Assam), he is a member of any of the Scheduled Tribes, whether of that State or of any other State (excluding the tribal areas of Assam), and is an elector for any Parliamentary constituency;
c. in the case of a seat reserved for the Scheduled Tribes in the autonomous districts of Assam, he is a member of any of those Scheduled Tribes and is an elector for the Parliamentary constituency in which such seat is reserved or for any other Parliamentary constituency comprising any such autonomous district;
d. in the case of the seat reserved for the Scheduled Tribes in the Union territory of (Lakshadweep) he is a member of any of those Scheduled Tribes and is an elector for the Parliamentary constituency of that Union territory;
    - in the case of the seat allotted to the State of Sikkim, he is an elector for the Parliamentary constituency for Sikkim;

- in the case of any other seat, he is an elector for any Parliamentary constituency.

Some of the conditions laid out for disqualification in Representation of People Act (1951) are:

a. He/She must not have been convicted for any offence that results in imprisonment for two or more years. However, detention under preventive detention law is not disqualification.
b. He/She must not have failed to lodge an account of election expenses within stipulated time.
c. He/She must not have any interest in government contracts, works and services.
d. He/She must not be a director or managing personnel in a company / organization in which government has at least 25% share.
e. He/She must not have been dismissed from government service due to corruption or disloyalty to state.
f. He/She must not have been convicted for promoting enmity between groups.
g. He/She must not have been punished for supporting social crimes such as untouchability, sati, dowry etc.

Further, Article 102 states that a person shall be disqualified for being chosen as, and for being, a member of either House of Parliament if:

a. He/She holds any office of profit under the government of India or the Government of any State, other than an office declared by Parliament by law not to disqualify its holder; The principle debarring holders of office of profit 'under the Government' from being a member of Parliament is that such a person cannot exercise his functions independently of the executive of which he is a part. The principle can be traced to developments in English constitution history, in the course of which it came to be established that the Crown and its officers shall have no say in Parliament.
b. He/She is of unsound mind and stands so declared by a competent court;
c. He/She is an undischarged insolvent;

d. He/She is not a citizen of India, or has voluntarily acquired the citizenship of a foreign State, or is under any acknowledgement of allegiance or adherence to a foreign State;

e. He/She is so disqualified by or under any law made by Parliament

If any question arises as to whether a member of either House of Parliament has become subject to any of the disqualifications mentioned in clause (1) of article 102, the question shall be referred for the decision of the President and his decision shall be final. Before giving the final decision, the President shall obtain the opinion of the Election Commission and shall act according to such opinion(Bakshi, 2008).

Apart from article 102, the Tenth Schedule to Constitution provides for disqualification of the members on ground of defection. Defection may be defined as abandonment of loyalty,duty or principle, or of one's leader or cause(Kashyap, 2008). It refers to defection of one's party in favour of an opposing one. A member may be disqualified if he/she voluntarily gives up the membership of his political party which gave him ticket to contest and win votes or abstains from voting in the House contrary to any direction issued by the political party to which he belongs, unless such voting or abstention has been condoned by the political party within fifteen days. A member elected as an independent candidate shall be disqualified if he joins any political party after his election. However, a nominated member is allowed to join a political party provided he joins such political party of his choices within a period of six months. After that period, joining a political party would lead to defection and disqualification(GK Today,2016). Indian politics have seen such defections very often. In between the fourth (1967) and fifth (1972) general election, out of 4000 odd members of the Lok Sabha and the Legislative Assemblies in the States and the Union Territories, nearly 2000 cases of defection were registered.

The question of disqualification on the ground of defection is decided by the Chairman in the case of Rajya Sabha (i.e. Vice-President) and Speaker in the case of Lok Sabha. The decision of Chairman / Speaker in this condition is subject to judicial review. Other conditions of vacating the seats apart from the disqualification grounds mentioned in Constitution, Representation of People Act (1951)and Tenth schedule, a member of parliament would need to vacate the seat in following circumstances:

a. A member of parliament can resign from his seat. The resignation letter is addressed to Chairman of Rajya Sabha (Vice-President) and Speaker of Lok Sabha.

b. The Chairman or Speaker can declare the seat vacated if a member has remained absent from all its meetings for a period of 60 days without permission. While calculating the 60 days, the period for which house is prorogued or adjourned is not counted.

c. If a member has been elected as President or Vice-President, or has been appointed as Governor of a state, his seat will be vacated.

d. A person cannot be come member of both Lok Sabha and Rajya Sabha at one time. If a person is elected from both the houses, he needs to intimate within 10 days to the house of which he desires to serve. However, if he fails to make such intimation, his Rajya Sabha membership will end. If a sitting Lok Sabha member becomes Rajya Sabha member or vice versa, the seat of former house will vacate.

e. If a person has contested elections on two seats and is elected on both, he needs to choose one. If he fails to do so, both the seats will get vacated. A person cannot be MLA and MP at the same time. If it happens that a person is both an MLA and MP, his MP seat will vacate.

Powers and Functions of Members of Parliament

The Constitution of India doesn't clearly enumerate the roles and responsibilities of members of Parliament but states the powers, privileges and immunities of Parliament and its members. As per article 105, the powers, privileges and immunities of members of Parliament are:

a. Subject to the provisions of this Constitution and to the rules and standing orders regulating the procedure of Parliament, there shall be freedom of speech in Parliament.

b. No Member of Parliament shall be liable to any proceedings in any court in respect of anything said or any vote given by him in Parliament or any committee thereof, and no person shall be so liable in respect of the publication by or under the authority of either House of Parliament of any report, paper, votes or proceedings.

c. In other respects, the powers, privileges and immunities of each House of Parliament, and of the members and the committees of each House, shall be such as may from time to time be defined by Parliament by law, and,until so defined(shall be those of that House and of its members and committees immediately before the coming into force of Section 15 of the Constitution(Forty-fourth Amendment) Act,1978.

d. The provisions of clauses(1),(2) and (3) shall apply in relation to persons who by virtue of this Constitution have the right to speak in, and otherwise to take part in the proceedings of, a House of Parliament or any committee thereof as they apply in relation to members of Parliament.

Article 105,Section 3 of the Constitution spell out the powers and privileges of MPs but the exact roles and responsibilities are not clearly defined. The Article states that " the powers of each House of Parliament and of the members and the Committees of each House,shall be defined by Parliament by law from time to time". The main role of MP is to perform legislative functions. Over the years, many executive functions are also carried out by MPs. The roles and responsibilities of MPs can be broadly classified into the following:

Legislative Role

The most prominent role of MPs is to make laws for the country. Article 245 and 246 defines the extent of laws made by Parliament and State Legislatures. As discussed earlier, the Seventh schedule distributes the legislative powers between the Union and the States. Parliament has the exclusive jurisdiction for making law for Union List and Concurrent list. Article 253 states that Parliament may legislate for implementing treaty or agreement with foreign country even though the matter falls in the State List. During President's rule under Article 356 or proclamation of Emergency under Article 352, Parliament can legislate in the State list. In this capacity, Member of Parliament make laws for governance of the country as enumerated in the Union list as well as Concurrent List. Members of Parliament also have voting rights for amendment in the Constitution of India subject to the basic structure. It is also the duty of Member of Parliament to discuss legislative issues like increasing or decreasing of state boundaries, change in the name of a State or Union Territories, determining jurisdiction of Supreme Court and High Court, creation of State Legislative Councils and also in the discussion and giving suggestions of a bill. Those Members of Parliament but not a Minister of the government can also propose legislative changes to the government through Private Members' Bills. Although, such bills are introduced in large number, it is hardly discussed and lapsed without even a single debate in the House. The Rights of Transgender Persons Bill,2014 was passed by the Rajya Sabha in April 2015 and it was the first private members' bill to get the approval of Rajya Sabha in the past 45 years. Member of Parliaments take part in the impeachment process of the President, removal of the Vice-President and judges of Supreme Court and High Court (The Hindu, 2015).

There is a provision of delegated legislation in Indian Parliament. Since, members of the Parliament has no time to carry out the detailed process once a bill is passed, executive are delegated to do so. Thus, a Member of Parliament has to keep monitoring the work of the executive and ensure that the powers of delegated legislation are not breached.

Accountability of Government

Members of Parliament are elected by the people to represent them in the Parliament. The members make law for the governance of the country. The execution and implementation of law is the responsibility of the executive. The role of Members of Parliament doesn't end at making law. It is also their responsibility to control and seek accountability of the executive. There are various mechanisms to monitor and supervise the working of the executive. It includes Parliamentary Committees, Question Hour, Calling Attention Motion, No-Confidence Motion, Zero Hour, etc.

Parliamentary Committees: Members of Parliament play an important role in monitoring and supervising the executive through various committees which will be explained in the later chapters.

Question Hour: It is the first hour of a sitting session of Parliament designated to questions raised by Member of Parliament pertaining to administrative activity of the government. The concerned Minister is obliged to answer such questions raised in the Parliament.

Calling Attention Motion: A Member of Parliament has the power to call for attention of a Minister. It can be on issues pertaining to the concerned Ministry which require urgent notice.

No-Confidence: A Member of Parliament can move a no-confidence motion to express lack of confidence in the government. In such case, the government have to prove the

Zero Hour: The question raised in the Parliament needs prior notice of not more than 21 days and not less than 10 days. In case, such notice could not be sent and the matter is of utmost importance, then Member of Parliament can raise the issue. So, immediately after the question hour that is about 12 noon, such questions are taken up. This hour is called Zero hour.

Electoral Role

Member of Parliament elects the President and the Vice-President of the country. Members of Lok Sabha elect the Speaker and the Deputy Speaker of the House. Similarly, member of Rajya Sabha elects the Vice-Chairman of Rajya Sabha.

Monitoring of Public Funds

Members of Parliament play a vital role in controlling public finance. Budget is an annual financial statement of the government which has to be passed by the members. No new taxes or modification of the existing taxation policies can be made without the approval from members of Parliament. It is also a mechanism to control spending of public funds by executive. Other mechanisms to control are through Committees like Public Accounts Committee, Committee on Public Undertakings and Estimates Committee.

As a Representative of the People

Members of Parliament are elected by the people from various constituencies. They represent the voice of the people from the constituency. So, they raise the concerns, issues, grievances of the people of his/her constituency. They also try to grab the attention of the government on serious issues. They try to point out the lapses on the part of government in the implementation of government schemes, programmes, policies, etc.

Members of Parliament Local Area Development Scheme (MPLADS)

MPLADS was announced on the 23rd December, 1993 by Government of India. The objective of the scheme is to enable Member of Parliaments to recommend works of developmental nature with emphasis on the creation of durable community assets based on the locally felt needs to be taken up in their Constituencies. Right from inception of the Scheme, durable assets of national priorities viz. drinking water, primary education, public health, sanitation and roads, etc. are being created. Some of the important features of the scheme are:

1. The MPLADS is a Plan Scheme fully funded by Government of India. The annual MPLADS fund entitlement per Member of Parliament constituency is Rs. 5 crores.
2. Lok Sabha Members can recommend works within their Constituencies and Elected Members of Rajya Sabha can recommend works within the State of Election except as provided in paras 2.8 and 2.9. Nominated Members of both the Rajya Sabha and Lok Sabh can recommend works anywhere in the country.
3. A Member of Parliament shall give his choice of Nodal District in Annexure I of the guidelines to the Ministry of Statistics and Programme Implementation with copy to the State Government and to the District Magistrate of the chosen District. If a Lok Sabha Constituency is spread over more than one District, the Member of Parliament can choose any one of the Districts as Nodal District in his/her constituency. The Rajya Sabha MP can choose any District in his/her State of Election as Nodal District. Nominated Members of both Rajya Sabha and Lok Sabha can choose any District in the country as Nodal District.
4. All works to meet locally felt infrastructure and development needs, with an emphasis on creation of durable assets in the constituency are permissible under MPLADS

Members of Parliament are part of the parliamentary democracy and represent the people of India. Even if, there is no codified powers and functions of members of Parliament, their responsibility is to carry out the functions of Parliament. They are responsible for the governance of the country. Their role is of immense importance in policy making, raising the needs and issues of the people, monitoring the functioning of executives, seeking accountability of the government and ensuring the development of the country.

Powers and Functions of Members of Legislative Assemblies

India is governed by three-tiered federal structure. The union government is at the apex, the state is second in the tier followed by local level governance of the Panchayats and Municipalities. The State legislature has been vested with powers to govern the state. The state legislature includes the Governor of the State and the Legislative Assembly known as Vidhan Sabha. Some states in India have bicameral structure of legislature. In such states, there is an upper house known as legislative council or Vidhan Parishad. Till 2017, there are seven states which have a bicameral structure. The states are Andhra Pradesh, Bihar, Jammu & Kashmir, Karnataka, Maharashtra, Telangana and Uttar Pradesh. Under Article 169, the decision to recommend to Parliament or to abolish Legislative Council in states where it exists and establishment of one where there is no Legislative Council, if the Legislative Assembly of the State passes a resolution to that effect by a majority of the total membership of the Assembly and by a majority of not less than two thirds of the members of the Assembly present and voting. Such kind of legislation is passed by simple majority and is not considered as an amendment of the Constitution.

Composition of Legislative Assembly:

The members of Legislative Assembly are elected directly by the people of the state from territorial constituencies, who exercise universal adult suffrage. The members in Legislative Assembly should not exceed 500 and not less than 60 members. The strength of members varies from 60 to 500 depending on the population of the state. For states like Arunachal Pradesh, Sikkim and Goa, the minimum number of members is fixed at 30 and for Mizoram it is 40 and Nagaland it is 46. Also, in Sikkim and Nagaland, some of the members are also elected indirectly. Further, the governor can nominate one member from the Anglo-Indian Community, if the community is not equally represented in the assembly. Initially this provision was to operate for ten years i.e. till 1960. This was supposed to be extended by 10 years each time. According to 95th Amendment Act, 2009, this provision will now continue until 2020. Similarly, there is provision for reservation of seats for Scheduled Castes and Scheduled Tribes in the assembly of each state on the basis of population. This provision was meant to be in vogue for ten years i.e. till 1960. The duration has been extended continuously since then by 10 years. This reservation will also last until 2020 with the 79th Amendment Act, 2009.

Like the Lok Sabha, the legislative assembly is not a continuing chamber. Its normal term is five years from the date of its first meeting after the general elections. The expiration of the period of five years operates as automatic dissolution of the assembly. However, the governor is authorized to dissolve the assembly at any time (i.e., even before the completion of five years) to pave the way for fresh elections.

Like Rajya Sabha, Legislative Council is a permanent body. It is a continuing chamber and one-third of its members retire every two years. The vacant seats are filled by newly elected and nominated candidates. The retiring members are eligible for re-election and re-nomination for any number of times. The members are elected for six years.

Eligibility of Members of Legislative Assembly

The qualification of member of legislative assembly or council is quite similar to the qualifications for members of Parliament. The eligibility of a person to be member of legislative assembly is laid down by the constitution in Article 173 are as follows:

1. He/She is a citizen of India, and makes and subscribes before some person authorized in that behalf by the Election Commission an oath or affirmation according to the form set out for the purpose in the Third Schedule.
2. He/She is, in the case of a seat in the Legislative Assembly, not less than twenty five years of age and in the case of a seat in the Legislative Council, not less than thirty years of age; and
3. He/She possesses such other qualifications as may be prescribed in that behalf by or under any law made by Parliament

The Parliament has laid down additional qualifications in the Representation of People Act, 1951(GoI, 1951)

1. To be qualified as member of the Legislative Council, he/she must be registered as a voter in an assembly constituency in the concerned state and must be eligible to vote. To qualify for the governors' nomination. He/she must be a resident in the concerned state.
2. To be qualified as member of the Legislative Assembly, he/she must be registered as a voter in an assembly constituency in the concerned state and must be eligible to vote.
3. If a person wants to contest a seat reserved for scheduled caste or scheduled tribe, he/she must be a member of scheduled caste or scheduled tribe. He/She can also contest a seat not reserved for them.

There are certain conditions laid down by the Constitution for disqualification of being a member of the legislative assembly or legislative council of a state:

(a) if he holds any office of profit under the Union or state government (except that of a minister or any other office exempted by state legislature),

(b) if he is of unsound mind and stands so declared by a court,

(c) if he is an undischarged insolvent,

(d) if he is not a citizen of India or has voluntarily acquired the citizenship of a foreign state or is under any acknowledgement of allegiance to a foreign state, and

(e) if he/she is so disqualified under any law made by Parliament.

Accordingly, the Parliament has prescribed a number of additional disqualifications in the Representation of People Act (1951) which are quite similar to those mentioned above for Member of Parliament.

Powers and Functions of Legislative Assemblies

The legislative Assembly enjoys the position similar to that of the Lok Sabha at the Union level. The members of the State Legislative Assembly elect a Speaker and Deputy Speaker who has the same position and function as the Speaker and Deputy Speaker of Lok Sabha. The State Legislative Council has a Chairman and Deputy Chairman elected by the Council similar to the Rajya Sabha at the Union level. The powers and functions of legislative assembly can be categorized under the following head.

Legislative Power

The Legislative Assembly is the highest law - making organ of the State. The Constitution endows the member of legislative assembly to make laws for items listed in list II of the Seventh Schedule known as the State List. The State List includes matters like public order, police, local government, public health and sanitation, agriculture, water, etc. Both the Union and State government has the power to legislate on matters listed in the Concurrent list which includes criminal law, preventive detention, marriage, divorce, bankruptcy, forest, economic and social planning, etc. In case of conflict between the two, the Union government prevails. When emergency has been imposed on the State, the Union government can legislate on subjects in the State List. The powers of members of the Legislative Assembly are the highest law-making organs of the State government but their powers are not absolute.

In a bicameral State, the Upper House i.e. Legislative Council cannot initiate money bills. However, ordinary bills can be raised in either of the House. The Legislative Assembly States where there is unicameral, all bills in the State list are initiated and passed by the House before sending for the Governor's assent.

Executive Power

The members of the State Legislative Assembly exercise executive power by controlling activities of the Chief Minister and the Council of Ministers. The Chief Minister and the Council of Ministers are answerable to the Legislative Assembly for its actions taken and not taken. There is a provision of "Vote of No-Confidence" which can be passed only by the MLAs in any state that, if passed by a majority can compel the government in power to resign. Similarly, there are other provisions like Question Hour, Cut Motions and Adjournment Motions to restrict the executive organ.

Financial Power

The financial power of Legislative Assembly is absolute in a State. All the expenses incurred by the executive have to be approved by the members of the Legislative Assembly. A money bill can be introduced only in the Legislative Assembly in states which have bi-cameral legislature. A majority of the members of the Legislative Assembly have to pass the Money Bill for expenditure of the Executive. In bi-cameral state, the Legislative Council can pass the Bill or suggest changes to the Bill within 14 days of its receipt. However, the members of Legislative Assembly are not bound to make the changes suggested. All taxation and grants proposals must be authorized by the members of the Legislative Assembly before it is implemented.

Electoral Power

The elected members of the Legislative Assembly form the Electoral College that elects the President of India. The members also elect the members of Rajya Sabha representing the particular State. The members have the electoral power to elect the Speaker and Deputy Speaker of the Legislative Assembly. Similarly, the members of the Legislative Council elect the Chairman and Deputy Chairman of the Legislative Council. In states with a bicameral legislature, one-third of the members of the Legislative Council are elected by the members of the Legislative Assembly.

Apart from the above powers, the members of the Legislative Assembly have the power to ratify some parts of the Constitution of India that relate to federal provisions like distribution of legislative and executive powers between the Union and the States, changes in 7th Schedule of the Constitution, any changes in Article 368 itself, etc. after such Bills are passed by the Parliament by special majority, needs ratification of more than half of the State legislatures, the State Legislative Council incase of bicameral State.. The members of the Legislative Assembly appoint various Committees to the House and also review the reports of the Public Service Commission and the Accountant General.

Conclusion

Originally, the Constitution of India has provision for two-tier system of government. The Union government at the Centre governs the entire nation and the State government governs the states. Afterward, a third tier of federalism was added in the form of Panchayati Raj at rural level and Municipalities at the urban level, which will be explained in the chapters for Local governance. Each tier has its own jurisdiction and powers to carry out their functions. The power of the Union government prevails in case of emergency or conflicts.

Review Questions:

1. Who can become a member of Parliament?
2. What are the powers, privileges and immunities of members of Parliament?
3. How members of Parliament do hold the executive accountable for their responsibility?
4. Write short note on MPLADS.
5. Explain the functions of members of Legislative Assembly.

References:

1. Bakshi, P.M.(2008) "The Constitution of India", Universal Law Publishing Company Private Limited, Delhi.
2. G K Today(2016) "Members of Parliament: Qualifications and Disqualification".Available at: http://www.gktoday.in/blog/members-of-parliament-qualifications-and-disqualification/(Accessed on 15/12/2017)
3. Government of India (1951) "The Representation of The People Act, 1951", Government of India. Available at:http://lawmin.nic.in/legislative/election/volume%201/representation%20of%20the%20people%20act,%201951.pdf
4. Kashyap, Subash. C.(2008) "Our Political System", National Book Trust, New Delhi, India.
5. The Hindu(2015) "Rajya Sabha passes Bill on Transgender Rights", 24th April,2015. Available at: https://www.thehindu.com/news/national/rajya-sabha-passes-private-bill-on-transgenders/article7138056.ece

THREE

Rural and Urban Local Self-Governance

Dr. Simer Preet Kaur

In a large democratic country like India, powerful central and state governments make good policies for all their citizens, but ensuring their implementation becomes a difficult task without the active participation of people at the grassroots level. Centralized planning cannot fulfill all the requirements and needs of people living in small, localized areas, which have specific issues or problems that need to be dealt with. This difficulty can be overcome with the implementation of decentralized planning and governance.

Decentralisation or self-governing institutions at local level are a prerequisite for good governance. Local governance, which can also be described as 'grassroots of democracy', is essential for socio-economic growth at the local as well as national level. Democratic decentralization is a process by which decision-making can be made by the people for themselves. They can resolve their problems, and participate in better-informed decision-making. It is an instrument for ensuring popular participation by people, engendering a sense of responsibility and promoting democratic values.

Decentralization also provides an enabling environment for area specific planning, where there can be close coordination between development schemes and local issues. This can also be described as democratization of development process with active participation of people. Decentralization helps to make development work smoother in all stages of implementation: in appraisal of the needs of the people, in assembling local resources, reducing local resistance, and speeding up of work with support of local people by ensuring their cooperation.

Historical Overview of Development of Local Governance in India

The consideration of units of local governance in India is not a novel concept. Decentralization in India began with the Panchayats, which had five village elders for settling disputes, leading the village towards betterment and also acted as village representatives for appealing to higher authorities whenever the need arose. These were custom based and tradition bound institutions which were mostly static. Even in the Mughal period, in spite of radical political changes, the institution of Panchayats continued with little or no change.

The British Period

The next stage in the evolution of local governance took place under the British rule in India. During the early stages of the British rule, it was the precedence of events and certain requirements, which resulted in the enactment of a system of local administration. In 1870, Lord Mayo introduced a decentralization scheme, which made provisions for local funds to be raised locally by Municipal and rural boards to meet their local requirements. (Mishra, 1983)

Lord Ripon's Reforms

The next important step was taken in 1882, with the resolution of Lord Ripon, who is called the father of local self-government in India. He worked towards financial decentralization, and local self-government reorganization in India. The local bodies act came into effect in, 1885. It was a step towards achieving decentralization through local bodies. This scheme envisaged that the smallest administrative unit, the taluka or the tehsil should be placed under a local board. District boards were to be constituted above these local boards in the provinces with powers of co-ordination. These local bodies were also to be given wide budgetary freedoms for financial decentralization.

Royal Commission on Decentralization

The royal commission on decentralization was set up in 1907 and submitted its report in 1909. After reviewing the workings of the local and district boards in numerous provinces of the country, they came to the conclusion that these boards were unrepresentative and inadequate for local governance.

The commission recommended that the people should be encouraged to participate in village affairs and to associate with local governance. They said that, "it is most desirable, alike in the interest of decentralization and in order to associate the people with the local tasks of administration that an attempt should be made to constitute and develop village Panchayats for the administration of local village affairs." (Malviya, 1965)

Government of India Resolution of 1918

A systematic effort was made by the British government in India to build up the institution of local government. The government of India act, 1918 provided for the majority of members of local and district board to be elected, which reinforced the democratization of these bodies.

Despite these measures being taken, the institutions of local governance could not develop as autonomous bodies, their constitution suffered from weaknesses and they lacked authority. The local self-government was made a transferred subject under the Montague-Chelmsford reforms of 1919. A large number of acts were passed by the provinces for the establishment of village Panchayats. These included:

1) Bengal village self-government act, 1919
2) Bombay and united provinces village Panchayat act, 1920
3) Assam rural self-government act, 1929
4) Punjab village Panchayat act, 1935
5) Karauli village Panchayat act, 1939
6) Hydrabad village Panchayat act, 1940
7) Mewar Gram Panchayat act, 1940 etc.

Many other villages also adopted similar village statutory bodies, but these bodies were not reflective of democratic spirit as most of its members were not elected representatives of people, but were appointed by the government,

Mahatma Gandhi's Vision

Mahatma Gandhi's vision for Indian democracy was that of the bottoms up approach. He wanted the entire structure of Indian democracy should be based on 'one popular election to the village Panchayat, indirect election from the village Panchayat to the state assemblies and from state assemblies to the Parliament' (Raghunandan, 2012), when the Constituent Assembly was set up, this Gandhian scheme of village Swaraj did not find many supporters in it. An overwhelming number of those present in the assembly, wanted to continue the '1935 act's pattern of leaving it to the states to establish and empower local government.' (Raghunandan, 2012).

Subsequently an amendment was moved by Gandhian, K. Santhanam, who believed very strongly in the concept of village Swaraj, and as a result, article 40 was inserted into the constitution. It dealt with organization of village Panchayats in part IV, which is The Directive Principles of state policy. The article reads, 'the state should take steps to organize village Panchayats and endow them with such power and authority as may be necessary to enable them to function as units of self-government' However, this provision stayed advisory in nature, and was not applicable by law.

Community Development Program(CDP)

A rural reconstruction program was launched by the government of India shortly after independence, which aimed at social and economic transformation of villages through active people's participation. The community development program (CDP) was launched in 1952 with an objective of providing socio-economic benefit to the rural poor. For the very first time an organized administrative set up was provided at the block, district, state and national level for carrying out development programmes.

The CDP was additionally strengthened by the establishment of National Extension Service (NES) by the government. The NES was set up to, 'tackle the problems of growth and development at different local and functional levels" (Singh, Mishra, and Pratap, 1997)

This first step towards decentralization and local governance was not very successful as it lacked the active and voluntary participation of people for whom the service was started. Lack of involvement and participation proved to be the biggest obstacle in successful implementation of both the CDP and the NES. The programmes did not pay adequate attention to the objective of developing 'responsible and responsive leadership' (Aslam, 2007) and thus became a program largely 'run by bureaucracy without local level participation.' (Singh, Mishraand Pratap, 1997).

Balwant Rai Mehta Committee

In January 1957, a study team on community development and projects and National Extension Service was set up under Balwantrai G. Mehta. The report prepared by this committee heralded modern India's first Panchayati Raj system. The committee observed that "development cannot progress without responsibility and power. Community Development can be real only when the community understands its problems; realizes its responsibilities; exercises its necessary powers through its chosen representatives and maintains a constant and intelligent vigilance on local administration." (GoI,1957)

The committee offered two broad guiding thrusts: First they stressed on the point that there should be decentralization of the administration for effective implementation of development programmes, and secondly that the administration should be under the control of elected bodies. The committee also proposed a three tier structure of the Panchayati Raj Institutions in India; at the village level there should be a Gram Panchayat, at the block level there should be a Panchayat Samiti, and at the district level there would be Zila Parishad. All three tiers of local governance should be linked with each other with genuine transfer of power. The committee reports quote that, "The team felt that in this way Panchayati Raj system would be able to establish a link between the people and the government" (Aslam, 2007)

Accepting the recommendations of the committee, a few states adopted Panchayati Raj system based on the three-tier formula. The system was initiated in the Nagaur district of Rajasthan on 2nd October, 1959. It was followed closely by states of Andhra Pradesh and Tamil Nadu. Between 1959-64, many other states also adopted Panchayati Raj Institutions (PRI) based on the three tier structure.

The PRI's thus created could not develop the democratic thrust and momentum needed for their success. It failed to cater to the needs of rural poor and was beset with problems. The active participation of people which is one of the necessities of any local governance was not forthcoming, and it became centers of power for a few local elites, with links to state and central governments.

Ashok Mehta Committee

The Ashok Mehta Committee was appointed in 1977, to review and recommend changes in the structure and functioning of PRI's. The committee addressed the issue of consolidation of local governance across the country. Observing that, "the story of Panchayati Raj has been the story of ups and downs" (the Ashok Mehta committee 1978, kurukshetra, vol-xxxvii), it categorized the development of local governance in india into three distinct phases; 1) first phase of ascendency from 1059-64. 2) The second phase of stagnation from 1965-69, and the 3) third phase of decline from 1969-71.

In its report, the committee listed several reasons for the stagnation and decline of PRI's in India; they include interference from bureaucracy, and government, lack of popular public participation and lack of financial resources.

Most importantly, the committee suggested a two tier composition of PRI's in India. They recommended setting up Mandal Panchayats, comprising of a group of villages at the block level and above it at the district level a Zila Parishad, the work of the Panchayat Samitis set up at block level till now, would be taken over by the Mandal Panchayats. At the basic village level, people would be involved with the Mandal Panchayat through constituted village committees.

These recommendations were adopted by the states of Karnataka, Andhra Pradesh, and West Bengal. The most important weakness of the committee's recommendations was that it lapsed the most basic grass root level organization of the Gram Sabha, or village Panchayat. At a Chief Ministers' conference in 1979, the majority of states rejected the two tier system and favored the continuation of the three tier structure of PRI's (Aslam, 2007) with the change in government in 1980, the recommendations of the report were not accepted.

G.V.K. Rao Committee

A Committee on Administrative Arrangements for Rural Development and poverty alleviation (CAARD) was set up in 1985 to review the various aspects of PRI's. This was also known as G.V.K. Rao committee after the name of its chairman. The committee observed that there is an urgent need for decentralization at the district level, saying that, "states have been generally lukewarm to the process of democratic decentralization. In most states the Panchayati Raj bodies have been allowed to languish without power and resources" (GoI, 1985)

The report also suggested the strengthening of Zila Parishads at the district level, and observed that the district should become the basic unit for rural planning and program implementation. It should also be given additional functions which come under the state level in order for it to become a strong and autonomous body.

The report also highlighted the role of the Block Development Officer (BDO) and called the office the 'spinal cord' (Aslam, 2007) of the rural development process. The report laid stress of making the PRI's empowered by giving them all possible support and by conducting regular elections of all local bodies.

L.M. Singhvi Committee

The Committee for the Concept Paper on Panchayati Raj Institutions (CCPPRI), constituted in 1986, also known as the L.M.Singhvi committee. The committee stressed on the point that the concept of Poorna Swaraj cannot be complete without the inclusion of Gram Panchayats in it. They pointed out that all the former experiments in the PRI's could not be successful because they made the error of "devaluing and downgrading the role of these institutions as units of self-government and relegating them to a secondary position, harming and hampering both democracy and development". (extracts from reports on various committees on PRIs, kurukshetra).

In its report the committee stated that local self-government should be constitutionally recognized, stressing on the importance of Gram Panchayats as 'embodiments of direct democracy'. (reports on various committees on PRIs: kurukshetra). For democracy to work at the grass roots level, elections for these bodies should be held after the expiration of specified term, adequate financial resources should be made available for effective functioning, and those attached to political parties should be discouraged to participate in these bodies.

Sarkaria Commission

The Sarkaria Commission, primarily concerned with center-state relations, but also gave suggestions for working and strengthening of PRI's. The commission, however, did not support the view of the L.M. Singhvi Committee report that PRI's should be given constitutional status. (Singh, and Misra. 1993)

Apart from these committees, some other mentionable committees, which gave their suggestions for the strengthening of PRI's were: a sub-committee of the consultative committee of parliament under the chairmanship of P.K.Thungon in 1988, and a committee under V.N. Gadgil in 1989.

Even after appointing these committees at different times and the collective suggestions given by them, the PRI's were not able to acquire the position and dignity of being the representative bodies of the rural masses. The basic principles, like active public participation; devolution of financial resources; operational decentralization; well-defined spheres of action; timely elections; and representation of weaker sections, which make local governance effective, were lacking. The remedy for all these was grant of constitutional status to the units of local governance.

Constitutional Status

By the end of the 1980's, it was becoming clear that strong steps would have to be taken for the regeneration and revival of these units of local governance. The suggestion of granting constitutional status to the PRI'S emerged as the only way to save the institution. There was a vital need to enshrine the basic and essential features of PRI's in the constitution for them to work with certainty and strength. Local governance would only be able to work effectively and efficiently if it functions as the third tier, and an indispensable part of a constitutional government.

64th Amendment Bill

In 1989, the then prime minister Rajiv Gandhi tried to constitutionalize local governance by introducing the 64th amendments to the constitution bill. This bill provided for a three tier structure of PRIs: at village, block, and district levels; a five years' term for the Panchayats; and the constitution of a finance commission. The bill got a two-thirds majority in Lok Sabha, but was not passed by the Rajya Sabha.

In 1990, the National Front Government again tried to introduce the bill trying to give constitutional status to the PRI's. This bill provided for a Gram Sabha at the village level, and Panchayats at any other level, as the state legislature may divide. This bill assured the autonomy of the states. There was no need to adhere to the rigid three tier system, and every state would get the freedom to experiment with the structure of Panchayati Raj in their state. It provided for direct elections for village Panchayats, and for Panchayats at other levels there would be partly (50%) direct elections and partly by and other mode to be decided by state legislature. This bill also could not become a law as the 9th Lok Sabha was dissolved.

72nd Amendment Bill

The 72nd amendment bill was introduced by congress government in 1991. This bill provided for a single tier Panchayat at the village level and if it deems necessary the state legislature may provide for Panchayats at the intermediate or district level, or both. It also provided for direct elections for Panchayats at the village, and intermediate (if constituted) levels, and for district level the state legislature can decide on the way representatives are to be chosen. This bill was referred to a joint select committee of the parliament in December, 1991.

73rd Amendment Bill

After many failed efforts and experiments, the 73rd Constitutional Amendment bill was passed in the Lok Sabha in December, 1992, and in the Rajya Sabha on 23rd December 1992. The bill became a law with the president's assent on April, 20 1993, and came into effect from April 24, 1993. As per the Amendment part IX, The Panchayats was inserted into the constitution, and the Panchayats got the constitutional status that was required to add the third tier of local governance in the country.

The amendment required all the states to conform to the constitutional amendment within one year and to hold elections by April 1995.

The Provisions of the Panchayats (Extension to the Scheduled Areas) Act, 1996

The Provisions of the Panchayats (Extension to the Scheduled Areas Act) (PESA)was passed on 24th December, 1996. This act extends Part IX of the Constitution (with certain modifications and exceptions) to the Fifth Schedule Areas notified under article 244(1) of the Constitution. Presently there are 10 States which come under the fifth schedule. They are Andhra Pradesh, Chhattisgarh, Gujarat, Himachal Pradesh, Jharkhand, Madhya Pradesh, Maharashtra, Odisha, Rajasthan and Telangana.

Salient Features of the 73Rd Amendment

- Composition of Gram Sabha: an embodiment of democratic power at the village level, working as an active body for development and fulfillment of local needs.
- Panchayati Raj Institutions based on the three tier system: Panchayats to be constituted at the village, intermediate and district levels.
- Reservation of seats: the act provided for reservation of one-third of the total number of seats for SC, ST, and women.
- Composition of Panchayats: the act provides for direct election to the Panchayats. The chairperson of the village Panchayat is elected as per the procedures of the state legislature, and the chairpersons at intermediate and district level are to be elected by and from amongst themselves.
- Duration of the PRI's: All the Panchayats are constituted for a duration of five years. If the Panchayats are dissolved before the stipulated time, reelections are to be held within six months.

- State Election Commission: the state election commission is responsible for preparation of electoral rolls, the superintending, directing and conducting the election of all Panchayats in the state.
- Disqualification of members: the act provides for a provision for disqualification of members of Panchayats if for any act they are also disqualified for elections of state legislature.
- Finance Commission: the act provides for a constitution of a finance commission in every state for proper availability of funds and for commencing development activities.
- Power, Authority, and responsibility: the state legislature is instructed to endow the Panchayats with such power and authority, which can enable them in functioning as institutions of self-government.
- District planning committee: Article 243ZD calls for the setting up of a District Planning Committee for decentralized planning and to consolidate the plans and programs of Panchayats.
- Powers to impose taxes: the state legislature can authorize a Panchayat to levy, collect and appropriate taxes, duties, tolls, and fees as necessary.
- Audit of Panchayat accounts: the state legislature can undertake auditing of the accounts of Panchayats.

The 73rd constitution amendment act also inserted the 11th schedule into the constitution under article 243G. This contains a list of 29 subjects that come under the Panchayat Raj institutions or rural local government. These are:

- Agriculture, including agricultural extension
- Land improvement, implementation of land reforms, land consolidation and soil conservation
- Minor irrigation, water management and watershed development Animal husbandry, dairying and poultry
- Fisheries
- Social forestry and farm forestry

- Minor forest produce
- Small-scale industries, including food processing industries
- Khadi, village and cottage industries
- Rural housing
- Drinking water
- Fuel and fodder
- Roads, culverts, bridges, ferries, waterways and other means of communication. Rural electrification, including distribution of electricity
- Non-conventional energy sources
- Poverty alleviation program
- Education, including primary and secondary schools
- Technical training and vocational education
- Adult and non-formal education
- Libraries
- Cultural activities
- Markets and fairs
- Health and sanitation, including hospitals, primary health centers and dispensaries
- Family welfare
- Women and child development
- Social welfare, including welfare of the handicapped and mentally retarded
- Welfare of the weaker sections, and in particular, of the Scheduled Castes and the Scheduled Tribes
- Public Distribution System, and
- Maintenance of community asset

Structure and Functions of Different Levels of PRI

The Panchayati Raj institutions have a three tier structure with different levels; village, intermediate and district.

The Village Panchayat or the Gram Sabha

The village Panchayat is the basic unit of the three tier structure of PRI's. It constitutes a Gram Panchayat, whose members are directly elected by the people. The chairperson of the Gram Sabha is called a Sarpanch/Mukhia/ Pradhan/Adhyaksha, in some cases there is also a vice chairman called an Up Sarpanch. A Sarpanch has very important role in the functioning of a Gram Sabha. He supervises and co-ordinates various activities of Panchayats. Apart from a Sarpanch, there is a village level secretary and village level workers, who assists the Sarpanch in working of Gram Sabha. The village level worker is also called a Village Development Officer. The other members of the Gram Panchayats are also directly elected and all have tenure of five years.

Duties of the Sarpanch include conducting the meetings of Gram Sabha at least twice a year, to regulate the records of the meetings, to exercise supervision over all the officers of Gram Panchayats, conduct all correspondence on behalf of the Gram Sabha, to represent his Gram Panchayat in the Panchayat samiti at intermediate level, and to exercise any such power and duty assigned to them.

Duties of the village secretary include assisting the Panchayat in recording its proceedings, preparing budget estimates, and preparing notices etc.

The village level worker or the village development officer is a crucial link between Panchayats and Panchayat Samitis at block level. They help Panchayats in making agricultural plans, educate farmers about modern agricultural practices, to supervise all institutions under the Gram Sabha, and point out any irregularities in any work to the sarpanch, and helping farmers securing loans etc.

Functions of the Gram Sabha

The Gram Sabha provides the following functions:

- Developing local level plans-economic development and livelihoods in:
  - Agriculture and allied sectors
  - local manufacturing

  - co-operatives and other people's collectives
- Human Development- in sectors of
  - health including nutrition
  - education including skills
- Social Development-specially of the marginalized groups including
  - development of women and children
  - development of people with disabilities
  - promoting traditional knowledge
  - addressing issues like bonded labour, child labour, and trafficking of women etc.
- Provision of basic services- includes enhancement of services
  - water supply
  - sanitation
  - power supply
  - markets
  - streets and roads
  - burial ground/crematoriums
- Planning for poverty reduction and livelihoods
- Planning of natural resource management and protection of bio-diversity. Etc.
  - To make the Panchayats and Gram Sabhas units of self-governance, it is very important that there should be fiscal autonomy. Gram Sabhas were given the right to levy, collect, and appropriate taxes at the local level for effective mobilization of financial resources. Sources of the Panchayats' income are property tax, agricultural tax, vacant land tax, entertainment tax, fees on registration of vehicles, fines, and penalties imposed, education cess, loans (if granted) by state or central governments, contributions and grants made by central or state government, Zila Parishad, Panchayat Samiti, or any other local authority.

The Panchayat Samiti

The Panchayat Samiti is the intermediate level of the PRI's in India, and is operational at the block level. A block is a group of villages constituted together for development work. A Panchayat Samiti comprises of the sarpanch or head of all the villages falling under its jurisdiction, local M. L. A's of the area (they cannot hold any office in Panchayat Samitis), a couple of co-opted members from SC, ST and women, a member of the co-operative societies, and some elected members etc. the Samiti is elected for a period of five years, and is headed by the chairman called a Pradhan, and a deputy chairman called up Pradhan. The government also appoints an officer called the Block Development Officer (BDO), who looks after various development works undertaken by the Panchayat samiti.

The duties of the BDO include implementing various schemes for economic development of the area under their jurisdiction, implementing schemes for social justice, exercise general control over all officers and employees of the Panchayat Samiti, maintenance of accounts of the Samiti, drawing up of the budget of the Samiti, preparing annual reports and submitting it to the Zila Parishad. etc.

Duties of the chairperson or Pradhan of the Simitis include to convene and preside over the meetings of the Panchayat Samitis, making plans and proposals for various development programmes, exercise control over the BDO and his staff, representing the Panchayat samiti at the district level, a Pradhan is also the ex-officio chairman of all the committees of the Samiti.

Functions of the Panchayat Samiti

- To co-ordinate the activities of all the Panchayats falling under its jurisdiction
- To implement activities concerning the rural welfare and development in the field of agriculture, Animal Husbandry, Health and Sanitation, Elementary Education, cottage industries, social welfare etc.
- Development of cottage and small-scale industries, and the opening of cooperative societies.
- Planning, implementation and execution of various community development programmes

- Providing basic amenities like drinking water, roads, drainage systems, irrigation etc.

The Panchayat Samitis get their funds from various sources. It gets grants-in-aid and loans from the state government, funds are also allotted to the Samitis from the block budget, it receives share of land revenue from the state government etc.

Zila Parishads

The Zila Parishad is the last and at the apex of the three tier PRI's in India, it is constituted at the district level and overviews the development works of the entire district. All the representatives of the Panchayat Simitis are members of the Zila Parishad, there are some nominated members from the marginalized sections of society, members of the state legislature and parliament representing that district, and the district level officers of the development departments of the area. The chief executive officer is from the IAS rank and heads the administrative set up of the Zila Parishad. The members also choose a chairman and a deputy chairman from amongst themselves.

Functions of Zila Parishad

The Zila Parishad mostly performs supervisory functions over the Panchayat Simitis. The Zila Parishad also renders necessary advice to the Government with regard to the implementation of the various development schemes. All the development work in the district is monitored and controlled by this district body. It also approves the budget of the Panchayat Samitis, and also assists them in discharging their functions. Some other functions of Zila Parishad include:

- Agriculture :-
  - increase agricultural productions
  - adoption of improved agricultural practices
  - training of farmers;
  - land Improvement and soil conservation.
- Irrigation ground water resources and Watershed Development:-

  - construction, renovation and maintenance of minor irrigation works
  - development of ground water resources;
  - watershed development programmes.
- Horticulture: -
  - rural parks and gardens;
  - promotion of cultivation of-fruits and vegetables;
- Statistics: –
  - publication of statistical and other information relating to activities of Panchayat Samiti and Zila Parishad .
- Rural electrification including distribution of electricity.
- Distribution of Essential commodities.
- Soil Conservation: -
- Soil conservation measures;
- Animal Husbandry and Dairying: -
  - establishment of Veterinary Hospital and Dispensaries;
  - promotion of dairy farming, poultry and piggery;
  - prevention of epidemics and contagious diseases.
- Household and Small Scale Industries including food processing: -
  - identification of traditional skills in the locality and developing household industries;
- Organisation of training programme for craftsman and artisans;
- Organizing khadi, handloom, handicraft and village and cottage industries;
- Rural Roads: -
  - construction and maintenance of roads other than National and State Highway;
- Health and Hygiene: -
  - establishment and maintenance of hospitals, primary health centers and dispensaries

- Rural Housing: -
  - implementation of house building programmes in the districts
- Education: -
  - promotion of educational activities including the establishment and maintenance of primary and secondary schools;
- Social Welfare and Welfare of Weaker Sections: -
- educational facilities to the Scheduled Castes, and Backward Classes
- Poverty Alleviation Programmes –
- Planning supervision, monitoring and implementation of poverty alleviation programmes.
- Social Reforms Activities. etc.

For the effective implementation of these works the Zila Parishad the central and state governments allot funds to the districts. on the recommendation of the State Finance commission constituted under Article 243-I of the Constitution of India, The State Government allows a Zila Parishad to levy any tax, duty, fee, toll and cess which has not been levied by any Gram Panchayat or Panchayat Samiti. Zila Parishad may also borrow money from the State Government for any development project.

Urban Local Governance

Municipal governance or urban local governance in India can be traced back to the year 1687, when Madras Municipal Corporation was established. It was followed by the establishment of Calcutta and Bombay Municipal Corporations in 1726.

The 74th Constitution Amendment Act, 1992 has introduced a new **Part IXA** in the Constitution, which deals with urban local bodies. This amendment came into force on 1st June 1993. It granted constitutional status to the municipalities and brought them under the justifiable part of the constitution. All the States had to adopt municipalities as per system enshrined in the constitution.

Salient Features of the 74th Amendment Bill

- The act apportioned three types of local self-governing units for urban areas;
- A Nagar Panchayat for areas which are in transition from a rural area to an urban area
- A Municipal Council for a small urban area; and
- A Municipal Corporation for a larger urban area.
- The division between a "transitional area", "a smaller urban area" or "a larger urban area" is based on the population of the area, the density of the population, the revenue generated for local administration, the percentage of employment in non-agricultural activities, and the economic importance of an area.
- Composition of Municipalities: all seats are to be filled by direct elections, for which each municipality is divided into areas called wards. The state legislature can nominate member in the municipality
- Constitution of ward committees: in municipalities which have a population of over three lakhs, ward committees are to be made
- Reservation of seats: one third of total seats are reserved for the SC, ST, and women.
- Duration of Municipality: they are to be constituted for a period of five years, and if it dissolves before the expiration if the time, elections for the same to be held within six months.
- Disqualification of membership: a member can be disqualified if he is disqualified under any law made by state legislature
- Power to impose taxes and funds: they can levy and collect such taxes as are assigned to them by state legislature
- Finance Commission: The Finance Commission constituted under article 243-I shall also review the financial position of the Municipalities
- Account Auditing of Municipalities: the accounts of municipalities can be audited

- State Election Commission: state election commission will undertake the work of superintendence, direction and control of the preparation of electoral rolls for, and the conduct of, all elections to the Municipalities
- Committee for District Planning: every State will have a District Planning Committee to consolidate the plans prepared by the Panchayats and the Municipalities in the district and to prepare a draft development plan for the district as a whole.
- Committee for Metropolitan Planning: every metropolitan area will have a metropolitan committee, to to prepare a draft development plan for the metropolitan area as a whole

The 74th Constitution amendment act also inserted the 12th schedule into the Constitution under article 243W. This contains a list of 18 subjects that come under the urban local bodies. These are:

- Urban planning including town planning.
- Regulation of land-use and construction of buildings.
- Planning for economic and social development.
- Roads and bridges.
- Water supply for domestic, industrial and commercial purposes.
- Public health, sanitation conservancy and solid waste management.
- Fire services.
- Urban forestry, protection of the environment and promotion of ecological aspects.
- Safeguarding the interests of weaker sections of society, including the handicapped and mentally retarded.
- Slum improvement and up gradation.
- Urban poverty alleviation.
- Provision of urban amenities and facilities such as parks, gardens, playgrounds.
- Promotion of cultural, educational and aesthetic aspects.

- Burials and burial grounds; cremations, cremation grounds and electric crematoriums.
- Cattle pounds; prevention of cruelty to animals.
- Vital statistics including registration of births and deaths.
- Public amenities including street lighting, parking lots, bus stops and public conveniences.
- Regulation of slaughter houses and tanneries.

Structure and Function of Different Levels of Urban Local Bodies

The 74th constitution amendment act provides for three types of urban local bodies classified as a "transitional area", "a smaller urban area" or "a larger urban area". This distinction is based on several distinctions like, the population of the area, the density of the population, the revenue generated for local administration, the percentage of employment in non-agricultural activities, and the economic importance of an area.

Nagar Panchayats

The Nagar Panchayats are made in the transitional areas which are progressing towards becoming an urban area from a rural area. These areas have a population of more than 30,000 and less than 100,000 inhabitants. The head of a Nagar Panchayat is the president, and it has a vice-president and some ward members too. All members are directly elected by the people. Besides the elected members, the Member of the State Legislative Assembly (M.L.A) representing that area is also the ex-officio member of Nagar Panchayat. It also has a chief executive officer called a Block Development Officer (BDO).

The tenure of Nagar Panchayat has been fixed at 5 years. If a Nagar Panchayat is dissolved before the expiry of its term, its re-election has to be held within six months of the dissolution.

Main Functions of the Nagar Panchayats

Nagar Panchayats have both obligatory and discretionary functions. The obligatory functions include water supply, drainage, scavenging the streets, street lighting, prevention of diseases etc. the discretionary functions include education, socio-economic development, organizing fairs etc. apart from these functions, the Nagar Panchayat also keeps a check on the development works, and can enquire about the same from the chief executive officer. It keeps a record of births and deaths within its jurisdiction.

Duties of the Chief Executive Officer

Each Nagar Panchayat has one executive officer, appointed by the state government. They are responsible for overseeing the daily work of the Nagar Panchayats. All the other officers of the Nagar Panchayat are subordinate to this office. They can also assign duties to other officers as they deem fit.

Sources of Income of Nagar Panchayats

The chief source of income of Nagar Panchayats is through grants from state government. It also collects taxes on water, houses, markets, entertainment and vehicles paid by residents of the town

Municipal Councils

A Municipal Council is constituted for a small urban area, which has a population ofless than three lakhs. It constitutes of 15-50 elected members, who are directly elected from constituencies, called wards. Apart from the elected members, it also has 3 members of state legislation(MLA) representing the entire Municipality or a part of it. They become the ex-officio members of the Municipal Council. There are also 3 members, nominated by the government for their knowledge and experience in the Municipal Council. Provision is also made for reservation of one third seats for SC, ST and women.

For Municipal Council elections, the whole area is divided into constituencies called wards. One councilor is elected from each ward by direct elections. The members of the council elect a president and the vice president from amongst themselves. They are elected for a period of five years. The Municipal Councils also constitute ward committees and standing committees to increase the participation of local people. A ward committee can be made comprising of one or more than one wards.

The President

The President is elected from amongst the members of the Municipal Council. They also elect a vice-president. Both the president and the vice-president can be removed by the state government. The president convenes and presides over the meetings of the Municipal Council. He is empowered to take disciplinary action against a councilor if he deems it appropriate. As the presiding officer, he authorizes expenditure of the council. He is the chief spokesperson of the council, and represents the council on official occasions.

Executive Officer

A chief executive officer is appointed by the state government along with some other executive officers like the council Secretary, the Health Officer, the Municipal Engineer etc. the chief executive officer is the principal executive authority in the council. He supervises the municipal office and looks after all the development work in his area. It is his duty to prepare the municipal budget and present it to the council. He can also enter into contract on the behalf of the council. He oversees the expenditure of the Municipal Council, and is in charge of collecting taxes, funs, fees etc.

Functions of Municipality

The Municipal Council not only performs civic duties, but also play an important role in local development and implementation of development plans. Some of the functions of the Municipal Council are:

- Basic administration of Municipality
- Making laws regarding power and functions of standing committees
- Imposes and collects taxes, fees etc.
- Raises loans
- Urban planning/town planning
- Providing civic amenities
- Construction of roads and bridges
- Urban poverty alleviation, etc.

Municipal Corporations

The Municipal Corporations are the highest level of local government in India. It is created in cities with more than three lacks of population. It is set up under a special statute passed by the respective state's legislature, or in case of a union territory the power to set up a Municipal Corporation lies with the Union Parliament. Members of the Municipal Corporation are directly elected by the people for a period of five years and they are called Councilors. It also includes a few nominated members.

The councilors elect a Mayor, and a deputy Mayor from amongst themselves. They are elected for a period of one year, and their term is renewable. The Mayor presides over the meeting of the Corporation and looks after its work. The mayor acts as link between the municipal corporation and the state government.

A municipal commissioner is also appointed by the state government. He is an administrative officer, who looks after the affairs of the corporation. Apart from the Commissioner, other officers are also provided, like Health Officer, the Chief Engineer, Education officers, the Executive Officers and the Octroi Inspectors, etc.

Sometimes, in case of megacities like Delhi, and Mumbai, one Municipal Corporation is not enough, and so it is divided into different zones. For example, Mumbai has 6 municipal zones, and Delhi had trifurcated into three area Municipal Corporations (North Delhi Corporation, South Delhi Corporation, and East Delhi Corporation).

The Municipal Corporations also make standing committees for various subjects like education, health, finance etc. One or more than one ward within a corporation can have their own administrative body known as ward committees.

Functions of Municipal Corporations:

The Municipal Corporations perform a variety of functions; Some are obligatory functions which include providing civic amenities like Supply of water, construction and maintenance of water works, electricity, transport, street lighting, cleaning public streets, public health and sanitation, preventive and curative measures for the good health of the people, immunization of children, setting up of hospitals and dispensaries, arrange for public safety by maintaining fire engines, ambulances.

Apart from these obligatory functions, the Municipal Corporation also performs some discretionary functions like building and maintaining public parks and gardens, to arrange for toilets, bathrooms, bathing ghats, washing ghats, etc., constructing and maintaining theatres and stadiums, planting of trees, registration of marriages, organization and management of fairs and exhibitions, Maintain rest houses, night shelters, children's homes, orphanages, Senior citizens homes, home for destitute women, etc.

Sources of Income

The main source of income for Municipal Corporations are grants from the government, loans approved by the state or central government, collection of various taxes like Property tax and toll tax on use of roads and bridges, Tax on vehicles, parking places, markets and hawkers, Octroi duty on goods brought into the city, Entertainment tax etc., Income from water and electricity supply, Income from the sale of Municipal or Corporation land, and Income from rents of the property of the Municipal Corporation.

Other Municipal Bodies

There are other local bodies which exist in other areas. Its nature and ways of functioning differ according to the population and area. The following are other municipal bodies which exist:

Notified Areas

A notified area is any area held in reserve by legal provision for future development. The term is also used for a village or a settlement with a population between 10,000 and 20,000. Any area which has a population of over 20,000 is called a town. Each notified area elects a notified area committee for its administration. All the members of Notified area committee as well as the chairman of the committee are nominated by the state government.

Town Area Committee

A Town Area Committee is a semi municipal authority constituted for small towns. Its members may be partly elected and partly nominated or wholly nominated or wholly elected by the state government. Town area committees perform a number of civic functions. The Rural Urban Relationship Committee,1966, suggested that smaller Town Area Committees should be merged with Panchayati Raj bodies, to make them units of self-government.

Township

A Township comes into existence when government sets up Public Sector Undertakings, and housing colonies are set up around them for the staff. The townships draw people from rural as well as urban areas and this develops into a kind of a very small town These townships are administered by the Municipal corporation or Municipality under which it falls.

Cantonment Board

Cantonment boards are set up in cantonment areas, where a Military station is established. These boards are centrally administered by the Defence Ministry. It consists of elected as well as nominated members and the officer commanding the station is the President of the Board.

Conclusion

The 73rd and the 74th amendments to the constitution were a great step forward for local self-government at the grass roots level. It gave power to the people to choose their representatives and strengthened the local governance in India. "These reforms aimed at devaluation of power, and social justice" (Kaur, 2016) These reforms brought about a wide spectrum of socio-political reforms in India. Politically empowered PRIs, with elected representation to the three tiers of PRIs and representation for scheduled castes(SCs)/ scheduled tribes (STs) as well as women, has been resolutely established.

For effective devaluation, the state governments should devolve functional autonomy, administration and financial resources to the PRIs, but this has not been happening. There is also a need to strengthen the District Planning Committees and capability development at all PRI levels. Another area where progress needs to be made is the financial resources of PRI's. The sources of revenue and other financial provisions allocated to Panchayats are far from adequate. This makes the PRI's reliant on the states for their finances, which makes them dependent on them, and thus they cannot function as autonomous bodies.

Review Questions:

1. Critically evaluate the role and functions of Panchayati Raj Institutions(PRI) in India.
2. What is the composition and main features of urban local government in India?
3. Trace the evolution of Panchayati Raj Institutions in India.
4. Examine the main features of the $73^{rd.}$ and 74th amendment act of the constitution.
5. Write short notes on:
    a) Gram Sabha
    b) Municipal Councils
    c) Zila Parishad
    4) Nagar Panchayat

References:

1. Aslam, M (2007). "Panchayati raj in India." National Book Trust, New Delhi
2. Bakshi, P.M., (2010). "Constitution of India." Universal Law Publishing, New Delhi
3. Government of India, (1985) "Report of the Committee To Review The Existing Administrative Arrangements For Rural Development And Poverty Alleviations Programmes" Ministry of Rural Development,Government of India
4. Government of India, (2016) Ministry of Panchayati Raj, "Revised Mandate of Ministry of Panchayati Raj" http://www.Panchayat.gov.in/documents/10198/456811/Book_Mandate%20of%20MoPR%20%2813.04.2016%29%281%29.pdf (accessed on 11/2/17)
5. Government of India (1957) "Committee on Plan Projects: Study Team (chairman: Balwantrai G. Mehta)." Planning Commission, New Delhi

6. Government of India, (2002-2007). "Planning Commission, Mid-Term Appraisal Of The Tenth Five Year Plan.", Planning Commision, Government of India http://planningcommission.nic.in/plans/mta/midterm/english-pdf/chapter-17.pdf (accessed on 13/2/17)
7. Kaur, Harpreet, (2016). "Governance: Issues and Challenges", Kitab Mahal, New Delhi
8. Kurukshetra, (1989). "Extracts From Reports of Various Committees on PRI's –the Ashok Mehta committee 1978" Panchayati Raj Review and Evaluation,vol-xxxvii, no.5
9. Kurukshetra, (1989). "Revitalization of PRIs for Democracy and Development, L.M.Singhvi Committee: 1986. Extracts From Reports on Various Committees on PRIs",
10. Malviya, H. D., (1965). "Village Panchayats in India." Economic and Political Research Department, All India Congress Committee, New Delhi
11. Mishra, B.B., (1983). "District administration and rural development." Oxford University Papers, New Delhi
12. Public Administration, (2012). "Urban Local Government: Municipal governance" http://publicadministrationtheone.blogspot.in/2012/09/urban-local-government-municipal.html (Accessed on 10/2/17)
13. Raghunandan, T. R., (2012). "Decentralization and Local Governments: The Indian Experience.", Orient Black Swan, New Delhi
14. Singh, S.S., Mishra, Suresh, and Pratap, Sanjay, (1997). "Legislative status of Panchayati Raj in India." Indian institute of public administration, New Delhi
15. Singh, S.S., and Misra, Suresh, (1993). "Legislative Framework of Panchayati Raj in India" Intellectual Publishing House, New Delhi.

Four

Supporting the Legislative Process

Ms. Paromita Datta

The Indian political system is based on the Parliamentary Form of Government both at the Centre (Article 74 & 75) and the State (Article 163 & 164) level as laid down in the Constitution with separation of powers among the three organs - the executive, the legislature and the judiciary. This division of powers elucidates the federal character of the Indian political system. Indian Parliament constitutes of the President of India along with the two Houses- the upper house known as the Rajya Sabha or Council of States and the lower house known as the Lok Sabha or the People's House. Though the President of India is not a member of Parliament, but she/he is an integral part of it. Thus, the Indian Parliament is bicameral in nature with two houses. The Indian Parliamentary system is based on the Westminster model followed in the United Kingdom, the framework for which was worked out by the Constituent Assembly of India. The democratic values and traditions found in the Indian political system can be traced back to the ancient period. Assemblies in the form of *Sabha* and *Samiti* have existed for a very long period. These assemblies represented the grass root democratic traditions prevalent within the ancient political system of our country and played an important role in the ancient political system.

The Regulating Act of 1733 was the first step towards establishing control of the British government over India. The beginning of the modern-day legislature can be traced back to the Charter Act of 1833 which established the legislative council for the entire British India. The Act of 1858 passed the control of the East India Company to the British Parliament, thereby ushering the era of Parliamentary control over the administration of the country. The modern democratic traditions and institutions in the country was a gradual process which stemmed from the struggle against the British rule in the country (Narain, 2007). The 1919 Montague-Chelmsford Act introduced bicameralism in the country. The gradual reforms and experiments from the Montague-Chelmsford Act of 1919 onwards moved towards the establishment of representative institutions in the country.

The Parliamentary system of our country reflects the democratic values and ethos of our country. The Parliament of India has evolved into a multidimensional institution reflecting and piloting the changes brought about by new and complex challenges. The Parliament plays an important role in steering social change through progressive legislations. Representing the will of the people through their representatives, the Parliament is destined to govern the basic norms of functioning of various other institutions, in addition to exercising the control over the executive to ensure its accountability. (Chakrabarty & Pandey, 2008).

How a Bill Becomes a Law

The Parliament of India performs various essential functions including the law making which is deemed to be the most important function of all. The Constitution of the country denotes Parliament as the highest law-making body. The Legislature is empowered to make laws on the subjects enumerated in the Union list and the Concurrent list contained in the seventh schedule of the Constitution. The Union list contains 97 items, whereas the Concurrent list contains 52 items. The Parliament is empowered to make laws on subjects mentioned in the State list under certain special circumstances, for example Emergency. Article 245 of the Constitution defines the scope of the territorial limits of the legislative powers vested in the Parliament and the legislatures of the States, whereas article 246 defines the respective jurisdictions of the Union and State Legislatures regarding their subjects of legislation.

Types of Bill: from Proposal to Act

Every legislative proposition known as the Bill can be initiated by either of the Houses in the Parliament except in the case of Money Bill or Financial Bill which can originate in Lok Sabha only. A Bill is a statute in draft and cannot become a law unless it has received the approval of both the Houses of Parliament and the assent of the President of India. Any Bill introduced by a Minister is referred as the Government Legislative Business. Whereas any Bill moved by any member of the Parliament (ruling party or opposition) is called as a Private Member Bill. Before a Bill can be sent to the President for his or her assent, it has to undergo several rigorous procedures.

The Bills originating in the Parliament can be broadly classified into three categories:

i. Ordinary Bill

ii. Financial Bill

- Money Bill
- Other Financial Bill–Category I & II

iii. Constitutional Amendment Bill

Table: 1

Type of Bill	Subject	House	Procedure of Passing
Ordinary Bill	Any item under the Union or Concurrent list	Can be introduced in any of the Houses.	Simple majority in both the Houses.
Financial Bill • Money Bill	Related to revenue and expenditure. Involves subjects related to taxation, government spending, withdrawal of Money by the govt. from the consolidated funds of India or Contingency Fund of India.	Can be introduced in Lok Sabha only.	Simple majority in Lok Sabha. The Rajya Sabha can recommend changes after consideration, but it is Lok Sabha's prerogative to accept or reject the changes. The Rajya Sabha must return or pass the Money Bill within 14 days or it is deemed passed.

• Category I	Contains items mentioned in Art. 110 along with other legislative matters.	Can be introduced in Lok Sabha only	Simple majority in both the Houses.
• Category II	Provisions related to expenditure from the consolidated funds of India. None of the items included in Art. 110 are part of it.	Can be introduced in either of the Houses of Parliament.	Simple majority in both the houses. But the President has to recommend it, only then the Bill can be passed by the Parliament.
Constitutional Amendment Bill	Amendments to the provisions of the Constitution.	Can be introduced in any of the Houses.	Requires simple majority of total members and two-third majority of the members present and voting. Some constitutional amendment Bills require ratification by the state legislatures as well.

Before a Bill can be introduced in any House of the Parliament, a notice pertaining to the motion signed by the minister or the member concerned has to be submitted to the office of the Secretariat. In the case of Lok Sabha, the notice regarding the motion has to be sent seven days in advance, however there is no such requirement for the Rajya Sabha.

1. Ordinary Bill:

An Ordinary Bill can be introduced in any of the two Houses of Parliament and it does not require the prior permission of the President. Provisions regarding ordinary Bill are enumerated in Article 10 of the Constitution. Both the Houses of Parliament have equal legislative authority over ordinary Bill. An ordinary Bill can either be introduced by a minister or by any member of Parliament. The Bill has to pass through various stages before it can become a law and has to undergo three stages of reading in each of the Houses.

First Reading: This is the first stage of the legislative process. It starts with the member in charge of the Bill asking for leave to introduce the Bill in the house. If the leave is granted, then the Bill can be introduced in the house. At the time of introduction, if the Bill is opposed by any member of the Parliament on the grounds that the said legislation is outside the purview of the House, the speaker might give permission for discussion. The question is put to vote of the House thereafter. During such discussion the speaker may give permission to the Attorney General to be present during the proceedings of the House. Once the Bill has been introduced, it is published in the Gazette of India. It can be published in the Gazette of India before its introduction if the speaker gives the permission to do so. In such cases, the leave to introduce the Bill in the house is not asked for and it can be introduced directly. Once the Bill has been introduced, it can be referred to the Standing Committee. The Committee considers the general principles and clauses of the Bill and submits its report to the house (for further details pertaining to Standing Committee and Committee System refer to the chapter on Committee System).

Second Reading: This is considered to be the most elaborate and vital stage in the life of a Bill because it is at this stage that a Bill receives a detailed examination (Kashyap, 2015). This part of the process can be divided into two sections: Stage I and Stage II.

- Stage I: At this stage a general discussion on the Bill takes place highlighting the basic principle underlying the Bill. At this point, the Bill can be referred to a Select Committee of the house or to a Joint Committee of both the Houses. The procedure for consideration of the Bill is the same in both the Houses. The House can also circulate the Bill to elicit opinions. In such cases the Bill is sent to the State governments and Union territories for publication in their Gazettes. The main purpose is to elicit opinions from the local bodies, various institutions, organizations and individuals concerned with the provisions of the Bill. Once the opinions are received, these are laid on the Table of the House followed by a motion for reference of the Bill to a Select Committee or Joint Committee. When the Bill is referred to the Committee, a detailed clause by clause examination of the contents is done. The Committee has the power to amend the provisions of the Bill but without changing its underlying principles. Once the Committee completes its work, it submits its report to the House.

- Stage II: After the Committee has submitted its report to the house a motion is moved for clause-by-clause consideration of the Bill by the house. During the discussion each and every clause of the Bill is taken up separately by the house and is also voted upon. At this stage amendment's in the provisions of the Bill can be moved by the members, and if they are accepted, they become part of the Bill.

Third Reading: Once all the clauses are considered and voted upon, the Minister in charge can move the Bill. At this stage, the discussion is generally confined to either in support of the Bill or for its rejection as per the directions given in the rule 94 of the Lok Sabha. For the passage of an Ordinary Bill simple majority of the house is required, i.e., member present and voting.

Bill in the Second House: The process of passing the Bill is the same in both the Houses. When the Bill is referred to the second house, it once again goes through the process followed in the first house, i.e., first reading, second reading and third reading. The second house at this point may consider any of the following options:

i. Passing the Bill without any amendments.

ii. Passing the Bill with amendments.

iii. Rejecting the Bill in totality

iv. Does not take any action pertaining to the Bill and thus keeping it pending.

If the second house passes the Bill without any amendments, then it can be sent to the President for his or her assent. But if the second house amends any provision of the Bill, it can be either accepted or rejected by the first house. If the amendments are accepted, the Bill is considered to be passed. But in case the first house rejects the amendments proposed by the second house, the Bill is sent again to the latter to get its consensus. If the second house insists on the proposed amendments, then a situation of deadlock arises between both the Houses. If the second house does not take any action for six months, then also a deadlock emerges between both Houses.

Joint sitting of both the Houses: During a deadlock, the President is empowered by the Constitution to summon a joint sitting of both the Houses. The deadlock occurs for three reasons:

i. If the Bill is rejected by the other House;
ii. If there's a disagreement between both the houses regarding the amendments to the Bill;
iii. If more than six months have passed from the date of receipt of the Bill by the other House without passing it.

The joint sitting is presided by the Speaker of Lok Sabha and is governed by the Rules and the Procedures of the Lok Sabha. It should be noted here that the provision of a joint sitting of both the houses is applicable to Ordinary Bill & Financial Bill of category I & II. It is not applicable to Money Bill or Constitutional Amendment Bills. With regard to the Money Bills, Rajya Sabha does not have any powers, whereas in case of a Constitutional Amendment Bill, it has to be passed by both the houses separately. The Constitution specifies that during the joint sitting no new amendments can be proposed except in two cases:

i. Those amendments that have caused final disagreement between the Houses; and
ii. Those amendments that might have become necessary due to the delay in the passage of the Bill.

If the Bill has lapsed due to the dissolution of Lok Sabha, a joint sitting of both the houses cannot be called unless the President has already notified his intention for a joint sitting.

The decision is taken by a simple majority of the members present and voting. The quorum for a joint sitting is one-tenth of the total members of both the houses taken together. Here, the Lok Sabha has the advantage of numbers with 545 members compared to 245 members of Rajya Sabha. In 2002, the President had summoned a joint sitting of both the houses for the Prevention of Terrorism Bill.

President's Assent: A Bill can become a law only if it receives the assent of the President of India. When a Bill is sent to the President's signature he/she has three alternative courses of action:

i. Gives his/her assent to the Bill

ii. Withhold his/her assent.

iii. Return the Bill to the House for reconsideration

If the President gives his/her assent to the Bill, it becomes an Act. But if the President withholds his/her assent and the Bill doesn't become an act. This is called as Absolute Veto. Generally, this veto power is used in two cases: i.) in case of Private Member Bills; and ii.) with respect to government Bills if the cabinet has resigned after the Bill has been passed but before the President signs it. And the new cabinet suggests the President to withhold his or her assent. For example, in 1991, President R. Venkataraman withheld his assent to the Salary, Allowances and Pension of Members of Parliament Amendment Bill. Finally, on the last day before the dissolution of Lok Sabha, the Bill was passed without obtaining the previous recommendation of the President.

In case the President sends the Bill back to the Parliament for reconsideration, it is called as Suspensive Veto. If the Parliament passes the Bill with or without amendments recommended by the President, the Presidents can no longer withhold his/her assent to the Bill. This simply means that the President's veto has been overridden by the re-passage of the Bill by the Parliament.

If the President does not take any action regarding the Bill - neither gives his/her assent nor send it back to the Parliament, it is called as a Pocket Veto. The Constitution of India does not prescribe any time limit for the President with regard to his assent for the Bills presented to him/her. For example, the Rajiv Gandhi Government in 1986 had passed Indian Post Office Amendment Bill imposing certain restrictions on the freedom of the press. This move was widely criticized from all quarters. When the Bill was sent to President Giani Zail Singh, he exercised the Pocket Veto. It was only in 1989 after three years when Shri. R. Venkataraman became the President that the Bill was sent back for reconsideration.

Private Member Bill

A Bill which is introduced by a Member of Parliament who is not a minister is called as a Private Member Bill. The main purpose behind this type of Bill is to give proper representation to the various views on different subjects prevalent in the society, thus persuading the government to address these issues by formulating appropriate policies. Two and half hours are allotted every alternate Friday during the Parliament session for business related to the private member Bills. There is not much difference between a government Bill and private member's Bill with regard to the various stages through which a Bill has to undergo before it can become an act. On the allotted day the Bills are presented on a priority basis:

1. Bills in respect of which the motion is that leave be granted to introduce the Bill;
2. Bills returned by the President with a message under article 111 of the Constitution;
3. Bills which have been passed by the Lok Sabha and returned by the Rajya Sabha with amendments;
4. Bills which have been passed by the Rajya Sabha and transmitted to the Lok Sabha;
5. Bills in respect of which a motion has been carried that the Bill be taken into consideration;
6. Bills in respect of which the report of a Joint or Select Committee has been presented;
7. Bills which have been circulated for the purpose of eliciting opinion thereon;
8. Bills introduced and in respect of which no further motion has been made or carried; and
9. Other Bills.

If a Member of Parliament wishes to introduce a Bill in the Parliament, one-month notice has to be given to the Chairperson or the Speaker of the House. However, the Chairperson or Speaker can waive this stipulation in certain cases and allow the Bill to be introduced with a shorter notice. The notice is to be accompanied by a copy of the Bill and an explanatory Statement of Objectives and Reasons. If a private member Bill in Lok Sabha seeks to amend any part of the Constitution, then it has to be referred to the Committee on Private Member Bills and Resolutions.

Once the Committee recommends the Bill only then it can be included in the list of business. The Committee also classifies the Bills according to their nature, urgency and importance into two categories: 'A' and 'B.' Bills classified under category 'A' have precedence over Bills under the category 'B.' Till now only 14 Private Member Bills have been passed. Since 1970 no Private Member Bill has been passed in the Parliament. In the 14th Lok Sabha 328 Private Member Bills were introduced, but only 14 were discussed by the House. In March 2016, Congress MP Sh. Shashi Tharoor sought to introduce a Bill on decriminalizing homosexuality in India by proposing an amendment in section 377 of the Indian Penal Code. However, as he sought the permission of the House to introduce the Bill it was opposed by BJP MP Sh. Nishikant Dubey, who demanded a division. The motion was put to vote by Speaker Smt. Sumitra Mahajan but it was defeated by 58 to 14 votes in the Lok Sabha.

2. Financial Bill

A Bill that deals with the subject of revenue or expenditure can be termed as Financial Bill. Financial Bill can be classified into three sections:

a) Money Bill
b) Category - I Article 117 (1)
c) Category - II Article 117 (3)

Money Bill:

A Money Bill is a specific kind of Financial Bill, which specifically deals with the matters specified in the Article 110. For Financial Bill to be presented as Money Bill, it has to be certified by the Speaker as a Money Bill. The Speaker has the final authority to decide and it cannot be challenged in any court of law. It is important to note that all Financial Bills are not Money Bill but all Money Bills are Financial Bills. For example, the Finance Bill introduced with the budget is considered to be a Money Bill because it contains provisions from the Article 110 (1).

Article 110 of the Constitution provides with the basic definition of a Money Bill. According to it, a Bill is deemed to be a Money Bill if it contains only the provisions dealing with all or any of the following matters (Bakshi, 2004), namely:

a. The imposition, abolition, remission, alteration or regulation of any tax;
b. The regulation of the borrowing of Money or the giving of any guarantee by the Government of India, or the amendment of the law with respect to any financial obligations undertaken or to be undertaken by the Government of India;
c. The custody of the Consolidated Fund or the Contingency Fund of India, the payment of Moneys into or the withdrawal of Moneys from any such fund;
d. The appropriation of Moneys out of the Consolidated Fund of India;
e. The declaring of any expenditure to be expenditure charged on the Consolidated Fund of India or the increasing of the amount of any such expenditure;
f. The receipt of Money on account of the Consolidated Fund of India or the public account of India or the custody or issue of such Money or the audit of the accounts of the Union or of a State; or
g. Any matter incidental to any of the matters specified in sub-clauses (a) to (f).

A Money Bill can only be introduced in Lok Sabha on the recommendation of the President and it can be introduced by the Minister only since it is considered to be a Government Bill. Once the Lok Sabha passes the Money Bill, Rajya Sabha can neither reject nor amend any provisions of the Bill. The Rajya Sabha has very limited power in this context. The Rajya Sabha has to return the Bill within 14 days of its receiving with its recommendation to the Lok Sabha. It is up to the Lok Sabha to decide whether to accept the recommendations of Rajya Sabha or not. In case the Rajya Sabha does not return the Money Bill within its stipulated time, the Bill will be considered passed by both the Houses once 14 days expire. Once the Bill is deemed passed by the Parliament it is sent to the President for his or her signature. The President can either give his/her assent to the Bill or can withhold it. The President cannot send the Bill back for reconsideration.

Category - I: Article 117 (1)

This type of Bill contains not only provisions mentioned in Article 110 but other legislative matters as well. For example, the Central Road Fund Amendment Bill, 2006 was introduced in the Parliament as Financial Bill - I. The Financial Bill category - I is similar to the Money Bill in two respects i) it can be introduced in Lok Sabha only, and ii) it can be introduced with the recommendation of the President only. Apart from these two exceptions the rest of the legislative procedure concerning such Bills is same as for Ordinary Bills. The Rajya Sabha can either reject or amend such Bills except that an amendment other than for the reduction or abolition of a tax cannot be moved in either House without the recommendation of the President. If there is a disagreement between both the houses regarding such Bills, the President is empowered to call for a joint sitting of both the Houses.

Category - II: Article 117 (3)

These are Bills related to the expenditure from the Consolidated Funds of India, but does not contain any item or matter mentioned in Article 110. These Bills are treated as Ordinary Bills and the legislative procedures concerning such Bills are same as for Ordinary Bills. The only difference is that they cannot be passed unless and until the President asks the Parliament to consider these Bills. For example, the President's (Emolument) and Pension Act can be considered to be a Bill of this category. This Bill contains provisions that money paid to the President of India as salary must be withdrawn from the Consolidated Funds of India.

3. Constitutional Amendment Bill:

Article 368 of the Constitutions empowers the Parliament of India to amend any provision of the Constitution without altering its basic structure. A Constitutional Amendment Bill can originate in any of the two houses of Parliament. The articles of the Constitution are divided in to three categories for the amendment purpose.

i. Bills requiring amendment by simple majority: As per Article 368, a Bill which seeks to amend any provision of the Constitution through a simple majority of members present and voting cannot be considered as a Constitution Amendment Bill. (Kashyap, 2015).

- Articles 2, 3 and 4: admission or establishment of new states, formation of new states, and alteration of areas, boundaries or names of existing States. Bills can be introduced in any House with the permission of the President. However, the President can ask for the views of the state governments, but is not bound to accept their recommendations.
- Article 169: creation or abolition of Legislative Councils in the States. If the Legislative Assembly of the concerned state passes a resolution with two-third majority of the members present and voting, then the Parliament can pass a law to do so.
- Para 7 of the Fifth Schedule: administration and control of scheduled areas and Scheduled Tribes.
- Para 21 of the Sixth Schedule: administration of Tribal Areas in the states of Assam, Meghalaya, Tripura and Mizoram.

ii. Bills requiring amendment by special majority: Bills seeking to amend all other provisions of the Constitution, including those enumerated in the article 368 (2) are called Constitution Amendment Bills. These Bills can also be introduced in either House of Parliament. Special majority means a majority of the total membership of that House and by a majority of not less than two-thirds of the members of the House present and voting. The special majority is prescribed for voting at the third reading stage as provided by the Rules of the House.

iii. Bills requiring amendment by special majority and ratification by States: Certain parts of the Constitution can be amended with the special majority along with ratification by the half the of State Legislatures before the Bill making provision for such an amendment is presented to the President for assent. The Constitution does not specify any time limit for the states to ratify such Bills. For example, the Goods and Services Tax Bill introduced in 2014 was finally passed by the Parliament in 2016. But this Bill required special majority and ratification by States.

- Election of the President (Article 54 and 55) The extent of the executive power of the Union and the States (Article 73 and 162)
- Supreme Court and the High Courts (Article 341, Chapter IV of Part V and Chapter V of Part VI of the Constitution)
- Distribution of legislative powers between the Union and States, or representation of States in Parliament (Chapter I of Part XI & 7th Schedule of the Constitution)
- The Procedure for the amendment of the Constitution (Article 368).

Lapse of Bill in Parliament

When the Lok Sabha is dissolved, all business, including Bills, motions, resolutions, notices, petitions pending before it or its Committees lapse. They must be reintroduced in the newly-constituted Lok Sabha to be pursued further. Articles 107 and 108 of the Indian Constitution enumerates the conditions and procedure regarding these provisions.

Cases When a Bill Lapse:

i. A Bill originated in the Lok Sabha but pending in the Lok Sabha.

ii. A Bill originated and passed by the Rajya Sabha but pending in the Lok Sabha.

iii. A Bill originated and passed by the Lok Sabha but pending in the Rajya Sabha.

iv. A Bill originated in the Rajya Sabha and returned to that House by the Lok Sabha with amendments and still pending in the Rajya Sabha on the date of the dissolution of Lok Sabha.

Cases When a Bill does not Lapse:

i. A Bill pending in the Rajya Sabha but not passed by the Lok Sabha.

ii. If the President has notified the holding of a joint sitting before the dissolution of the Lok Sabha.

iii. A Bill passed by both Houses but pending assent of the President.
iv. A Bill passed by both Houses but returned by the President for reconsideration of the Rajya Sabha.
v. Some pending Bills and all pending assurances that are to be examined by the Committee on Government Assurances do not lapse on the dissolution of the Lok Sabha.

During the 15th Lok Sabha a total of 68 Bills lapsed. Some of the important Bills that lapsed were: The Constitution (108th Amendment) Bill to reserve 50 percent of seats in Parliament and in the state Legislatures for women; The Constitution (110th Amendment) Bill, seeking to reserve half of the seats in the Panchayats for women; The Constitution (112th Amendment) Bill reserving one-third of elected seats in municipalities for women; The Judicial Standards and Accountability Bill, 2010 – meant to lay down standards of conduct for judges. As per the provisions of the Bill, it required for the judges and their families to declare details pertaining to their assets and liabilities.

Withdrawal of a Bill

The process of withdrawing a Bill can be initiated by the member in-charge of the Bill at any point on the grounds that:

i. The legislative proposal contained in the Bill is to be dropped;
ii. The Bill is to be replaced subsequently by a new Bill, which substantially alters the provisions contained therein;
iii. The Bill is to be replaced subsequently by another Bill, which includes all or any of its provisions in addition to other provisions; and if such leave is granted no further motion shall be made with reference to the Bill.

If a Bill is under consideration in a Select Committee of the House or in the Joint Committee of the Parliament, then any motion pertaining to the withdrawal of the Bill will be automatically referred to the Committee. Once the Committee expresses its opinion in the report, it can be included in the business list of the House. In case a Bill has originated in the Rajya Sabha and is pending before the Lok Sabha then the member in-charge has to move a motion in the Lok Sabha recommending to the Rajya Sabha to agree to the leave being granted by the Lok Sabha to withdraw the Bill and after the motion is adopted by the Lok Sabha and concurred in by the Rajya Sabha, the member in charge shall move for leave to withdraw the Bill.

If the motion for leave to withdraw a Bill is opposed the Speaker, if thinks fit, may permit the member who opposed the Bill and the member in-charge of the Bill to make brief explanatory statements and then it is put to vote without any discussion.

Subordinate Legislation

The functions of the modern state have increased to an enormous proportion. The state has to incorporate a vast number of activities within its ambit, touching almost all the aspects of human life. Today the legislative business of the government has not only increased, but has also become more complex. Due to its sheer size it is not possible for the government to devote adequate time to all the legislative matters. The Parliament of India officially meets three times a year. This limited time puts constraints and limitation on it's working. It is not enough time for Parliament to complete its task as a result more than often the legislations remain overdue to the extent that they lapse. The rules of procedure and conduct of business of both houses have provisions in subordinate legislation also known as delegated legislation. According to the principle of delegated legislation, the legislature must lay down guidelines, the principles and framework of the policies for the executive to make rules and regulations. The legislature often delegates its power to legislate to subordinate agencies as it frames laws in broad terms (an outlay) and the responsibility to provide details pertaining to the law rests with the Executive. The Executive has to work within a prescribed limit while the framing rules and regulation concerned with the legislation. The rules and regulations made by a subordinate agency within the ambit of the authority delegated by the legislature are called as subordinate legislation or delegated legislation. These rules and regulations are statutory in nature. According to M.P. Jain, "the term 'delegated legislation' is used in two senses: a) exercise by a subordinate agency of the legislative power delegated to it by the legislature or b) the subsidiary rules themselves, which are made by the subordinate authority in pursuance of the power conferred on it by the legislature."

Subordinate legislation has become an essential part of legislative business today. One of the arguments given in favor of subordinate legislation is that it plays an important role in times of emergency. In emergency conditions require immediate appropriate measures to effectively deal with the situation. Due to the nature of the working of the Parliament it is difficult for the legislature to deliberate and take fitting action concerning the situation. Many a time certain important matters of legislation require expert opinions. Therefore, it becomes a necessity that powers to deal with such matters is given to the appropriate administrative agencies to be exercised according to the requirements of the subject matter. Unforeseen circumstances encountered by Parliament often lead to difficulty while implementing certain decisions. There are various clauses in statutes containing a 'removal of the difficulty clause' which empowers the administration to remove difficulties by making rules and regulations which hamper the proper execution of legislative decisions. These clauses are always so worded that the powers given to the administration are extensive. Subordinate legislation saves Parliamentary time by performing the various tasks entrusted to it by the Parliament. It also gives an opportunity to engage experts associated with various fields, to have their valuable inputs as guidance during the drafting stage. Also, subordinate legislation provides greater degree of flexibility and can be easily changed according to the changing circumstances.

The legislature in India cannot delegate its essential legislative functions which include determination of legislative policy or enacting a policy. Subordinate legislation is subject to the Parliamentary control. Once the legislature delegates its powers to subordinate agencies it is important that after the rules are framed, the concerned departments refer it to the Ministry of Law and Justice for detailed evaluation from legal- constitutional aspect. The main functions of the Committee on Subordinate legislation of Lok Sabha are to examine: i) whether the rules are in accordance with the general object of the Act, ii) whether the rules contain any matter which could be dealt in a better way, iii) whether they are retrospective, iv) whether they directly or indirectly bar the jurisdiction of the court, and questions alike. A similar Committee exists in Rajya Sabha discharging the same functions as the Lok Sabha Committee.

Subordinate Legislation is often criticized on the point that this practice has led to the appropriation of legislative powers of the Parliament by the Executive. This has led to the increase in the powers of bureaucracy which is not responsible to the people of India. However, despite this drawback the importance of subordinate legislation has increased over the years. There are few mechanisms which establish control over such legislation so that the administration does not become arbitrary while formulating rules and regulations. The Judiciary in India has the power to review whether subordinate delegation is consistent with the 'Parent Act' or not. The validity of such legislations can be challenged on the ground that it is beyond the purview of the Legislature. According to Article 246 of the Constitution the judiciary is empowered to declare any Act passed by the Parliament on the grounds of excessive legislation. The parent Act may be Constitutional but the delegated legislation emanating from it may come in conflict with some provisions of the Constitution and hence it can be declared unconstitutional. The rules on the subordinate legislation of the Parliament prescribes that once executive frames rules related to Bill the Committee on subordinate legislation must lay it down before the House. The Committee on Subordinate legislation in the legislature exercises a very effective control over it. The functions of the Committee on Subordinate Legislation are to scrutinize and report to the House whether the powers to make regulations, rules, sub-rules, byelaws etc. conferred by the Constitution or delegated by Parliament are being properly exercised within such delegation. The Committee examines all rules, regulations, sub-rules, byelaws etc. Also, the Courts in India have upheld that the Subordinate Legislation cannot be enforced unless it is published. Subordinate Legislation is in no way less important than the principal law as it always carries with it the full force of the principal law.

Role of the Standing Committee

Modern Parliaments perform various roles. Their functions are no longer limited to only certain sectors but have increased to huge proportions which makes it difficult to manage the effectively the functions and responsibility entrusted to it. The complex nature of today's functions has made it nearly impossible for the Parliament to devote sufficient time for all its legislative functions. Over the course of time various mechanisms and tools have evolved through which the Indian Parliament fulfills its responsibilities. Committee system is one such mechanism which provides the parliament with necessary support required to complete its tasks. Ideally, Parliamentary Committees would be a venue for the consideration of legislation introduced in Parliament. The volume and complexity of legislation, the demands on the time of parliamentarians and Parliament's preoccupation with the politics of the moment make it difficult to give legislative business the attention it requires (Kapur & Mehta, 2006).

The origin of the Committee system in India can be traced back to the Constitutional Reforms of 1919. The Constitution of India makes a passing reference to Committee system, it does not make any specific provision with respect to Committee system. Standing Committee is a Parliamentary Committee constituted every year or periodically and works on a continuous basis. The Standing Committee system was established in the year 1993 on the recommendations made by the Rules Committee of the Lok Sabha. The department related standing Committees were increased from 17 to 24 in 2004. 16 departmental standing Committees come under the ambit of Lok Sabha whereas the rest of the 8-departmental standing Committee comes under the purview of the Rajya Sabha. After a Bill has been introduced in the Parliament, it can be then referred to the Standing Committee related to the subject matter of the Bill. However, it is not mandatory to refer the Bills to the Committee. The Government can either accept or reject the suggestions forwarded by the Standing Committee on the draft of the Bills. Many times, the reports of the Committees are not even laid on the Table of the House. During the tenure of the 15th Lok Sabha, almost 70 percent of the Bills were referred to the Standing Committee. Referring a Bill to the Standing Committee allows in-depth discussion and analysis of the Bill, which is not possible on the floor of the Parliament. This also gives an opportunity for creating consensus across party lines which makes the passage of the Bill easier. The members of the standing Committee do not belong to a particular political party, but represent all the parties present in the Parliament. These members not only belong to different political parties based in various regions of the country, but they also come from different strata of the society, thereby giving voice and representation to various divergent views pertaining to the subject matter of the Bill. The Members of the Committee while working on a particular issue gain expertise which enables them to make more informed contribution to Parliamentary debate, assessing legislation, and holding the government to account (Hudson, 2006). The Standing Committees play a very crucial role in the policy process by examining the Bill at its drafting stage before it could be laid down on the Table of the House.

Standing Committees can be classified according to their nature in 6 broad categories:

1. Financial Committees
2. Departmental Standing Committees (total 24 in numbers)
3. Committees to Inquire
4. Committees to Scrutinize and Control
5. Committees Relating to the Day-to-Day Business of the House
6. House-Keeping Committees or Service Committees (i.e., Committees concerned with the Provision of Facilities and Service to Members)

The Standing Committees play a very important and vital role in the legislative procedures in bringing about significant changes in policies. The role of the Standing Committees is to thoroughly review the Bill and recommend necessary changes. For example, the Standing Committee on Science and Technology examined the Civil Liability for Nuclear Damages Bill (2010) and made several key recommendations which resulted in the increase of the potential liability of suppliers of nuclear equipment in case of an accident. The nature of the Standing Committee reflects the work it is engaged in. The three Financial Committees, namely the Estimates Committee, the Public Accounts Committee and the Committee on Public Undertaking are considered to be some of the most important Committees of the Parliament. These three Committees scrutinize the Government finances, thereby keeping a check on the Executive. The Estimates Committee, for example, reviews whether the estimates laid out by the Government are in accordance with the rules and regulations, thus, reducing the scope of extravagant expenditure by the Government. The

Public Accounts Committee through its functions has the power to bring out the irregularities within the government finances.

The Committee on the reforms of the Indian Medical Council Act 1959 proposed for a new Act, replacing the existing IMC Act. It recommended complete overhauling and restructuring of the regulatory mechanism concerning medical education in the country. While the Committee reviewing the Bill pointed out the issues with the Medical Council of India, making appropriate suggestions for its improvements. The Standing Committee of Rajya Sabha on Health and Family Welfare agreed to a great extent with Dr. Ranjit Roy Chaudhury Expert Committee constituted in 2014 on the reforms pertaining to the MCI. Standing Committees through their work maintain the Parliament's accountability towards the people of the country. The Committees while examining the details of the Bills and legislations ensure that there is no breach of the limit set by the Parliament. The functions carried out by the Committee on Privileges are of semi-judicial in nature. It deals with questions relating to the privileges enjoyed the Members of Parliament. The Committee safeguards the powers and prestige of the Members. The Department related Standing Committees in principle under the law can review any aspect of the workings of a particular Ministry. The work carried out by various Standing Committees while examining a Bill brings out the lacunae within it. This provides an opportunity for the Government overcome the gaps remaining in the Bill.

Conclusion

The evolution of modern legislative practices in India evolved with the advent of the East India Company and subsequently the British Government at the beginning of the 17th century. The political, administrative and financial reforms meant to strengthen the British rule in India established the basic framework of legislature in the country. The Constitution of India provides for a Parliamentary form of Government for the whole of India. The responsibility of law making is the most important function of the legislature as it is the highest law-making body in the country. The different types of Bills originating in the Parliament reflects the demands and changing contours of the society in the country.

Since the time Constitution of India came into force on 26th Jan 1950, it has been amended 101 times to accommodate the transformation brought on by changing times. The functions and responsibilities of the Legislature have increased by leaps and bounds, which makes it difficult to devote sufficient time to all the legislative affairs. To provide assistance to the Legislature to complete its multiple tasks the role of Committees become very crucial. In the contemporary period Standing Committees provide strength to the Legislature. The Committees enables as the Parliament to carry out its function efficiently. However, it must be noted that though the Standing Committees perform a very important role in the legislative procedure, their recommendations are not binding.

Review Questions:

1. Explain the various types of Bills originating in the Parliament.
2. What is a Private Member Bill?
3. What is meant by Subordinate Legislation? What is its significance?
4. What role do the Standing Committees perform in the legislative process?
5. What is the difference between an Ordinary Bill and a Money Bill?

References:

1. Bakshi, P.M., (2010). "Constitution of India." Universal Law Publishing, New Delhi.
2. Burman, Anirudh, (2010), "Standing Committee Report Summary - The Civil Liability for Nuclear Damage Bill." PRS Legislative Research, New Delhi. http://www.prsindia.org/billtrack/the-civil-liability-for-nuclear-damage-bill-2010-1042/ Accessed on 12.01.2017
3. Chakrabarty, Bidyut & Rajendra Kumar Pandey, (2008), "Indian Government and Politics." Sage Publication India Pvt. Ltd. New Delhi.
4. Government of India, Ministry of Parliamentary Affairs, "Rules of Procedures & Conduct of Business in Lok Sabha." Accessed on 20.12.2016
5. Lok Sabha Secretariat(2014) "Rules of Procedures & Conduct of Business in Lok Sabha." Ministry of Parliamentary Affairs, 15th Edition, Government of India.

6. Government of India (2004). "Manual, Subordinate Legislation." Ministry of Parliamentary, Government of India Affairs. Available at http://www.mpa.nic.in/mpa/Manual/Manual_English/Chapter/chapter-11.html Accessed on 20.12.2016

7. Hardgrave, Robert L. (Jr.) & Stanley Kochanek, (2008). "India - Government & Politics in a Developing Nation" 7th Edition. Thomson Wadsworth

8. Hudson, Alan, (2006). "CSOs and Parliamentary Committees" Overseas Development Institute, UK www.odi.org, accessed on 24.12.2016

9. Jain, M.P., (1993). "Constitutional Law of India" Wadhwa Company Law & Publisher.

10. Kapur, Devesh and Pratap Bhanu Mehta, (2006). "The Indian Parliament as an Institution of Accountability". Democracy, Governance and Human Rights Programme Paper Number 23. United Nations Research Institute for Social Development https://casi.sas.upenn.edu/sites/casi.sas.upenn.../The%20Indian%20Parliament.pdf. Accessed on 10.12.2016

11. Kashyap S.C., (2015). "Our Parliament"National Book Trust of India, 5th Edition, New Delhi

12. Kumar, Rohit., (2010). "Vital Stats – Private Member Bills in Lok Sabha." http://www.prsindia.org/Parliamenttrack/vital-stats/private-members-bills-in-lok-sabha-2010-1011/ Accessed on 2.02.2017

13. Mahajan, V.D., (1986). Constitutional Development & the National Movement in India. S. Chand & Company, New Delhi.

14. Pandey, J.N., (1991). "Constitutional Law of India".Central Law Agency, Allahabad

15. Rao, Prianka, (2014). "Parliament as a Law Making Body." Background Note for the Conference on Effective Legislatures. PRS Legislative Research. http://www.prsindia.org/Parliamenttrack/discussion-papers/Parliament-as-a-law-making-body-3479/ Accessed on 12.02.2017

16. Pylee, M. V., (1995). "An Introduction to the Constitution of India." Vikas Publishing House, New Delhi.

17. Shankar, Apoorvaand Shreya Singh, (2015). "Parliamentary Procedures: A Primer – Rajya Sabha". PRS Legislative Research, Institute for Policy Research and Studies. New Delhi.http://www.prsindia.org/administrator/uploads/general/1425009754_Rajya%20Sabha%20Primer-%20Final.pdf Accessed on 12.03.2017

FIVE

Committee System in India

Dr. Radha Kumari

Parliamentary system in India has evolved for over 67 years now. Our political system has witnessed several important developments during this period, which have impacted practices and procedures of Indian Parliament. After independence, Indian constituent assembly adopted a system which could best guarantee democratic aspirations of its people. Knowledge and experience of working with Westminster model was another reason for choosing the Parliamentary system in India.

It would be erroneous to say that Indian Parliament is a replica of British Parliament, as Indian Parliament has its own sets of practices and procedures within the framework of Indian milieu. As far as experience is concerned, prior to 1947 Indian Legislature was equipped with only a few devices to raise matters. In the post-independence period, several new devices have enabled members of our legislature to draw attention of the Government, and to voice the grievances of people. A true test of parliamentary institution lies in its capacity to adapt, change, evolve and incorporate

Many important developments have been incorporated in the practices and procedures of Indian the Parliamentary system. On the one hand these developments have helped Parliament meet new challenges of the changing times; on the other hand, they have ensured better control and regulation over the Executive. One such development of vital significance is committee system in India, which also has undergone many changes since its inception.

Parliamentary Committees in India have proved to be the backbone of parliamentary power and autonomy. Department related standing Committees is a landmark development in this regard. How far this committee system has been effective in influencing the legislative work in India in comparison to some other countries can be an interesting topic for a comparative study.

Need of the Committee System

Parliament is a large body which is plagued by many issues, particularly now-a-days, like party politics, factionalism, policy dissention on vital issues of national interests and paucity of time; therefore, it is not able to perform its duties in a well organised manner. So, the actual work of Parliament, like regulation of Executive and administration, scrutiny of legislative and constitution amendment bills, etc. is done through these Parliamentary Committees rather than through the whole House. In fact, the efficiency of parliamentary regulation over Executive remains very much dependent on the efficiency of the work of these Committees.

Parliamentary Committees are the microcosms and extension of the whole House and much of the parliamentary business is conducted through these Committees only. These Committees perform the functions delegated to them by the House. Receiving information is the first essential need of the Parliament for effective discharge of its functions. These Committees help in finding out facts of cases, examining witnesses and evidences and then making reasonable recommendations. Parliamentary Committees assist the House in its principal task of ensuring executive accountability.

Need of the Parliamentary Committees can be summarised in a few points as below:-

- **Growing Responsibilities of Parliament**

  Modern state is now bound to ensure good governance to its people. So there are added responsibilities which Parliaments are now assuming. Police state is no more a norm now in this age of market. The unprecedented growth in Governmental activities has resulted in need of a strong and elaborate Committee system.

- **Changing Roles of Parliament**

  Modern Parliaments are not only taking up added responsibilities; their functions have become more complex also. In an age of communication technology, Parliament needs experts' advice on complex matters. Parliament cannot deal with such issues in the whole House. In Committees it is always easier to get consultation with experts on the subject and discuss the issues in good detail.

- **Shorter Sessions**

  During the period 1993-2003, the Rajya Sabha and the Lok Sabha sat for an average of 71 and 75 days in a year, accounting for about 348 and 433 hours respectively. There is a downfall in the number of sittings of these two Houses if we compare with their annual average for the previous five years from 1988 to 1992, which comes to 80 and 91 days, accounting for 515 and 595 hours respectively. It is precisely in this context that successive All-India Conferences of Presiding Officers have been expressing concern at the shrinking days of sessions in various Legislatures in India. As a result, important functions of Parliament, like scrutiny of legislative and constitution amendment bills, scrutiny of Budget, etc. are not done properly in the Houses. (Malhotra, 2004).

- **Disturbed Sessions**

  Indian Parliament and its State Legislatures are particularly plagued by this issue. In the recent time only, the whole winter session of December 2016 was sacrificed on the issue of demonetisation. And unfortunately this has become a trend in Indian Parliament to hold the whole session for political gains by political parties. As a fallout of it, Parliament which is supposed to have serious discussions and debates on the matters of public interest, turns into a battlefield. The need of Committee system is felt more in this regard as members of Committees are able to work across party lines.

Definition of Parliamentary Committee

According to Subhash Kashyap, "A Parliamentary committee in Lok Sabha, by formal definition, means a committee which is appointed or elected by the House in pursuance of a motion, or nominated by the speaker and which works under the direction of the Speaker and presents its reports to the House or to the speaker and the Secretariat for which is provided by the Lok Sabha/ Rajya Sabha Secretariat. But not every committee consisting of members of Parliament is a Parliamentary Committee. There are other Committees consisting entirely of members of Parliament, e.g., Consultative Committees attached to various ministries and departments, but they are not Parliamentary Committees" (Kashyap, 2012).

Origin of Committee System in India

Origin of the Committee system in India can be traced back to the days of British Rule in India under Charter Act of 1853 and Government of India Act 1919. (Kashyap, 2012). In 1950 when Indian constitution was first adopted, Committee system was incorporated in its original draft also. Since then the Indian constitution has evolved and undergone some transformations according to the changing circumstances. As a result, there was an increase in the number of Committees as well as in their functions and powers.

Types of Committees in India

According to Mr. G. C. Malhotra, former Secretary General of the Lok Sabha, Parliamentary Committees may be distinguished from Consultative Committees and Government Committees.

A Parliamentary Committee means a Committee which is appointed and elected by the House or nominated by the Speaker of Lok Sabha or Chairman of Rajya Sabha. It works under the direction of the Presiding Officer and presents its report to him or to the House. Its secretariat is provided by one of the two Secretariats.

Consultative Committees are constituted by the Minister of Parliamentary Affairs by nomination of members from both the Houses. The strength of these Committees is fixed by the Government in consultation with opposition parties with due regard to the respective strength of various parties in Parliament. The maximum membership of a Consultative Committee is 40. Consultative Committees are formed for the Ministries and Departments of the Government.

The Government Committees, Councils, Boards, etc. are constituted by the Government either in pursuance of statutes or by the Government resolutions on which Members of Parliament are represented. At present, there are 56 such Government Committees.(Malhotra, 2004).

There are two types of Parliamentary Committees in India, viz.

1) Standing Committees
2) Ad hoc committees

Standing Committees

Standing Committees are those which are constituted by the House or the Speaker every year or from time to time, as the case may be, and are permanent in nature in the sense that they examine different issues and present their reports to the House or Speaker from time to time during their term.

Standing Committees may be categorised in terms of the nature of their functions, as follows:

i. Financial Committees, e.g., Committees on Estimates, Committees on Public Accounts, and Committees on Public Undertaking.
ii. Subjects Committees or departmentally related standing joint Committees of the two houses.
iii. House Committees that are Committees relating to the day to day business of the house, e.g., Committees on absence of Members from the sittings of the House, Business Advisory Committees, Committees on Private Members Bill and Resolutions and Rules Committees.
iv. Enquiry Committees, e.g., Committees on Government Assurance, Committees on subordinate Legislation, Committees on Paper Laid on the Table and Committees on the welfare of Scheduled Casts & Scheduled Tribes.

v. Service Committees, e.g., General Purpose Committees, House Committees, Library Committees and Joint Committees on Salaries and Allowances of Members of Parliament.

Ad hoc Committees

Ad hoc Committees are appointed for a specific purpose and they become functus officio as soon as they have completed the task assigned to them and presented their reports.

Ad hoc Committees may be broadly put into two categories

i. Select or Joint Committees on Bills which are appointed to consider and report on particular Bills.

ii. Committees which are constituted from time to time to inquire into the report on specific matters. Thus, Railway Convention Committee is an Ad hoc Committee which is appointed from time to time to examine the finances of the Railways and to review the rate of dividend which is payable by the Railway undertaking to the General Revenues. (Kashyap, 2012).

Evolution and Growth of the DRSC System

The setting up of Department Related Standing Committees (DRSCs) in Parliament was the result of years of study of similar experiences in the Parliaments of United Kingdom, United States of America, Australia, etc., and extensive deliberations at various Parliamentary fora. (Malhotra, 2004).

Subject Committees

In India, a beginning in this direction was made in eighth Lok Sabha, on 18th August, 1989 with the setting up of three subject Committees, one each on; Agriculture, Science and technology and Environment and Forest, which were reconstituted in the Ninth Lok Sabha. The successful functioning of the three subject Committees i.e. Committees on Agriculture, Science and Technology and Environment and Forest during the period of over three years(1989-1992) led to the constitution of 17 Departmentally related Standing Committees on 8 April, 1993, covering under their jurisdiction all the ministries and departments of the Union Government.

Of the 17 DRSCs, 6 Committees (one each on Commerce, Home Affairs, Human Recourse Development, Industry, Science & Technology, Environment & Forests, Transport, and Tourism & Culture) were managed and serviced by Rajya Sabha Secretariat and 11 Committees (one each on Agriculture, Defence, Energy, External Affairs, Finance, Food, Civil Supplies and Public Distribution, Information Technology, Labour and Welfare, Petroleum and Chemicals, Railways, and Urban and Rural Development) were managed and serviced by the Lok sabha Secretariat. Each one of these Committees had 45 members – 30 to be nominated from the Lok Sabha and 15 from the Rajya Sabha. (Malhotra, 2004).

Restructuring of the Committee System

Over a period of time, it was observed that unwieldy jurisdiction of some of the DRSCs makes it difficult for them to examine and report on all subjects selected by them. It was also observed that the long time taken by some of the Committees in examining and reporting on the bills tend to delay their passage in Parliament. Taking all this into consideration, the Joint Parliamentary Committee on Jurisdictional overlap between Parliamentary Committees, in its report, presented on 26 July, 2001, recommended for restructuring of the Committee system. At the meeting of Speaker with the leaders of parties held on 4 July, 2004, it was agreed to raise the number of DRSCs from 17 to 24 as recommended by JPC on Jurisdictional overlap. The 24 DRSCs will have the same functions as are assigned to 17 DRSCs. Out of 24 Committees, 16 will be serviced by the Lok sabha secretariat while 8 by the Rajya Sabha secretariat. (Malhotra, 2004).

Structure of DRSCs was also changed. Now each DRSC will be formed with 24 members from the Lok Sabha and 10 members from the Rajya Sabha. With the restructuring of the system of DRSCs, while a few Committees were newly created, and a few were renamed according to the change in their jurisdiction. So far as the DRSCs managed and serviced by the Lok Sabha secretariat are concerned, five more Committees were created, thereby raising the number of such Committees from 11 to 16. Of these five Committees, four are newly created ones. They are Committees on Water Resources, the Committee on Chemicals and Fertilizers, the Committee on Coal and Steel, and the Committee on Social Justice and Empowerment. This apart, the Committee on Urban and Rural Development has been bifurcated creating two separate Committees-one on Urban Development and the other on Rural Development.(Malhotra, 2004).

In the process of restructuring of the system of DRSCs, three Committees have been renamed. The Committee on Food, Civil Supply and Public Distribution has been renamed as the Committee on Food, Consumer Affairs and Public Distribution; The Committee on Labour and Welfare has been renamed as the Committee on Labour; and the Committee on Petroleum and Chemicals has been renamed as the Committee on Petroleum and Natural Gas. The total number of Committees, managed and serviced by the Rajya Sabha Secretariat, has been raised from six to eight with creation of two more Committees-one on Health and Family Welfare, and another on Personnel, Public Grievances, Law and Justice.(Malhotra, 2004).

At present, there are 55 Parliamentary Committees. Among these 55 Committees, 31 are Joint Committees of both the Houses and 24 Committees are single House Standing Committees. Nine Committees, each in Lok Sabha and Rajya Sabha have similar functions in the respective Houses, e.g., Committee on Privileges, Committee on Petitions and Committee on Government Assurances etc.

Rajya Sabha has a provision of 3 Standing Committees, which are: Ethics Committee, the Committee on Provision of Computers for Members of Rajya Sabha and the Committee on the Members of Parliament Local Area Development Scheme. Such Committees with similar functions in Lok Sabha are constituted as adhoc Committees. In the same manner there are three Committees which exist only in Lok Sabha, which are as follows:

- The Estimates Committee
- The Committee on the Absence of Members
- The Committee on Private Members' Bill

Rajya Sabha is not associated with the Estimates committee as it does not have financial powers. Rest of the functions regarding absenteeism of members and private members' Bills are directly taken care of by the whole House in Rajya Sabha.

Composition and Working of Parliamentary Committees

All the 55 Committees are formed in proportion to the respective strength of the parties in Houses. Having all party composition, these Committees are different from party bodies which work in a partisan manner. During the conduction of inquiries, these Parliamentary Committees are able to operate across party lines. These features of Parliamentary Committees make their work more important.

Sittings of Parliamentary Committees are held in private. It is not permissible for a member of the Committee, or anyone else who has access to the proceedings of the committee, to communicate, directly or indirectly to the press, any information regarding its proceedings etc . before its report has been presented to the House. There are no public hearings before the Committees and the Press is not permitted. (Kashyap, 2012). Committees generally hold their sittings during sessions of the House, but are otherwise empowered to sit during the inter-session period. By reason of the prorogation of the House, any business before a Committee does not lapse and the Committee continues to function notwithstanding such prorogation. (Tyagi, 2004).

Generally, the chairman of the committee fixes the date and time for the sitting of a committee. But in case the chairman is not readily available, the Secretary General may fix the date and time for the sitting; but in case of a select or a Joint Committee on a Bill, he can do this only after consultation with the Minister in-charge of the Bill.

- **Annexure containing information about the membership, chairmanship and tenure and functions of these 55 Parliamentary Standing Committees is given at the end of the book.**

Proceedings in Committees

Proceedings in Committees are largely conducted in the same manner as in the House but in a more intimate and more informal atmosphere.

When a Committee is deliberating, a member can speak more than once on the question under consideration. After the Chairman is satisfied that sufficient discussion has taken place, he puts the question to the Committee and ascertains the decision. All questions at a sitting of a Committee are decided by a majority of votes of the members present and voting. Except in the case of Select or Joint Committees on bills, questions are not formally put to the vote of the Committee and as far as possible, unanimous decisions are taken. In rare cases, when there is difference of opinion in a Committee, either both opinions are included in the report of the Committee or a reference to the difference of opinion is recorded in the minutes of the Committee. A question, on which a Committee has already taken a decision, may be reopened at the same or a subsequent sitting of the Committee with the permission of the Chairman. (Kaul & Shakdhar, 2001).

Quorum

The quorum to constitute a sitting of a Committee is, as near as may be, one-third of the total membership of the committee. In special circumstances, the quorum to constitute a sitting of a Committee may, under the orders of the House of the Speaker, be reduced to less than one-third of the total number of members of the Committee. A convention has been established whereby a quorum of one-third of the total membership is not insisted upon at the sittings of the Committee when the witnesses are examined since no decisions are taken at such meetings

Reports

The Committees submit their reports to the Chief Presiding Officer of their House. These reports may be preliminary or final. The Committees may make special reports on any matter that arises or comes to their notice in the course of their work and which they may consider necessary to bring to the notice of the House. It is open to the House to discuss any of the reports presented to it by its Committee. Some reports it discusses and adopts. Other reports are not discussed at all. It all depends upon the subject matter of the report. However, the recommendations of the Committees are normally accepted by the House and implemented by the Government. In case there is a difference of opinion between a Committee and the Government, and it remains unresolved, the matter is referred to the House for final decision. The House in that case considers the alternate proposal of the Government as well, and then takes a decision. (Tyagi, 2004).

Powers of Committees

Powers of the Committees of the Lok Sabha have been laid down in the Constitution in rule no. 89 and the rule 90. According to rule 91, directions may be issued there by the Speaker from time to time. The powers which are generally possessed in common by all Committees of the Lok Sabha are briefly described in the following paragraphs.

i. **Power to Appoint Sub-Committees**

   A Committee, under rule 97, may appoint one or more Sub-Committees, each having the powers of the whole Committee, to examine matters which may require detailed study or investigation. In pursuance of this power, a number of Standing Committees, as also Select or Joint Committees on Bills, have appointed Sub-Committees from time to time for detailed study of specific matters to assist them in redrafting of particular clauses of a Bill.

   If the Deputy Speaker is a member of a Sub-Committee, he is *ex-officio* appointed Chairman of the Sub-Committee.

ii. **Power to Take Evidence or Call for Documents**

   A Committee, under rule 102, may take oral and/or written evidence or call for documents in connection with a matter under its consideration, examination or investigation.

iii. **Power to Make Special Reports**

   A Committee has the power to make special report on any matter that arises or comes to light in the course of its work which it may consider necessary to bring to the notice of the Speaker or the House, as the case may be.

iv. **Power to Pass Resolution on Matters of Procedure**

   Where a case warrants a special procedure for conducting the business of a Committee, that Committee may pass resolutions on matters of procedure relating to it for the consideration of the Speaker who may make such variations in procedure as he may consider necessary.

v. **Power to Make Detailed Rules**

With the approval of the Speaker, a Committee may make detailed rules of the procedure to supplement the provisions, for its internal working. (Kaul & Shakdhar, 2001).

Functions of Committees

Committees of Parliament perform different kinds of functions; whether these are Department related Committees or Subject based Committees. An account of their functions is given below:

Consideration over Demands for Grants

According to G. C. Malhotra, an important function for DRSCs of the Parliament is to consider the Demands for Grants of the concerned ministries and make a report on the same to the Houses. There is a bar that report shall not suggest anything of the nature of cut motions. The following procedure is prescribed to be followed by the DRSCs in their consideration of Demands for Grants:

a. After the general discussion on the budget in the House is over, the Houses shall be adjourned for a fixed period;

b. The Committees shall consider the Demands of the concerned Ministries during the aforesaid period;

c. The Committees shall make their report within the period and shall not ask for more time;

d. The Demands for Grants shall be considered in the Houses in the light of the reports of the Committees; and

e. There shall be a separate report on the Demands for Grants of each Ministry. (Malhotra, 2004).

No specific period is fixed in the rules for the adjournment of the Houses of Parliament for consideration by DRSCs of the Demands for Grants. However, since 1993, the Houses of Parliament have adjournment every year during the Budget session for a period of nearly four weeks to enable the DRSCs to consider the Demands for Grants of all Ministries of Government of India and finalise their reports. (Malhotra, 2004).

Each DRSC or Subject Committee scrutinises the Demands for Grants which fall in its purview. Since their aim of scrutiny is to ascertain economy and efficiency, their scrutiny is confined to variations in the Demands from the previous year, more particularly any increase. If any new expenditure is asked for by the Ministry for new services, these Committees review the relationship between the expenditure and the service.

Consideration Over Long-Term Policy Issues

The DRSCs review annual reports of the ministries and any long-term policy document which is referred to them by the Houses.

In terms of functioning, it can be easily concluded that a good deal of qualitative work is done by these Committees. Until 1993, Demands for Grants were used to be discussed in Lok Sabha only. There was no such provision to discuss them in dedicated Committees. As a result, demands for Grants of most of the Ministries used to get passed without any scrutiny, because the House could have discussed Demands for Grants only of a few ministries due to lack of time.

Legislative Work

Ministries generally refer the Bills to the concerned DRSCs for examination. The DRSCs have to follow a certain procedure for reviewing such Bills.

a. The Committee shall consider the general principles and clauses of the Bills.

b. The Committees consider only those Bills which are introduced in any of the Houses and referred to them by the Presiding officer of the concerned House.

c. The Committee has to make its reports on the Bills within the given time period.

Delegated Legislation

As this has been already discussed that Parliament faces paucity of time for a number of reasons, legislative work in good measure is delegated to its Committees. In the Parliament, there are Committees regarding Subordinate legislation in the Lok Sabha and Rajya Sabha both.

Measuring the Effectiveness of Committees

The effectiveness of such committees can be measured both quantitatively and qualitatively. One quantitative study, among many conducted during the period from 8 April, 1993 (in the tenth Lok Sabha) till 31 December, 2003 tells that 17 DRSCs had presented 1623 reports to the Parliament. Of these, 1079 were original reports on Demands for grants, Bills, Policies, Annual Reports/Subjects, and 544 were 'action taken reports' (Malhotra, 2004). How far these Committees have been able to influence the Government activities, particularly the financial decisions, is an issue for study.

According to Subhash Kashyap, the elaborate procedure for follow-up of the recommendations of these Committees by way of 'Action Taken Reports' is essentially an Indian innovation (Kashyap, 2012).

An analysis of the action taken by the Government on the recommendations made by 11 DRSCs of the Lok Sabha, from April, 1993 to December, 2003 is given below:

Total number of recommendations made	8756
Total number of recommendations accepted by the Government	4680 (53.45%)
Total number of recommendations which the Committees did not pursue in view of replies by the Government	1480 (16.9%)
Total number of recommendations in respect of Which replies have not been accepted by the government	(1541) (17.59%)
Total number of recommendations on which final replies awaited	1055 (12.04%)

Thus, while 53.45% of the recommendations have been accepted by the Government, the Committees did not pursue the matter in respect of another 16.90%. These figures prove amply the effectiveness of the system in ensuring accountability and responsiveness of the Executive to the Parliament. (Malhotra, 2004).

Chart 1: Acceptance rate of Committee recommendations

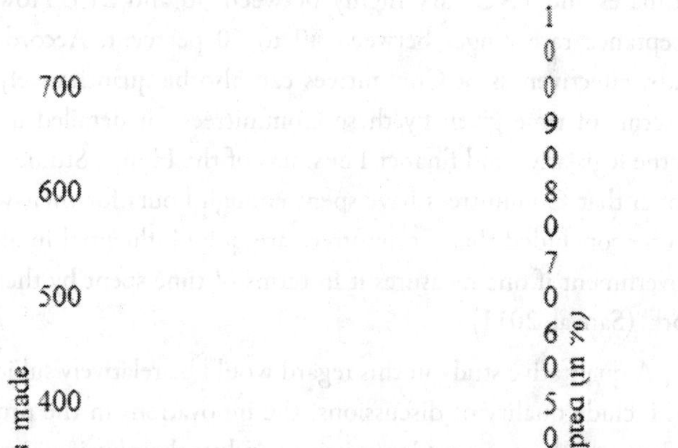

Source: Strengthening Parliamentary Committees Background Note for the Conference on Effective Legislatures

In Chart 1, graphic presentation of data has been used to throw some light on this aspect. This data does not include Bills since no Action Taken Reports are tabled regarding Bills. The Subordinate Legislation

Committee made 28 recommendations with an acceptance rate of 93 per cent. The DRSC on HRD, on the other hand, made 608 recommendations but the acceptance rate for these recommendations was only 7 per cent.

The number of recommendations in Committees on MPLADS, Estimates and PAC vary highly between 36 and 213. However, their acceptance rate ranges between 40 to 60 per cent. According to one study, effectiveness of Committees can also be quantitatively measured in terms of time given by these Committees for detailed deliberations on the legislative and financial business of the House. Studies have again shown that Committees have spent enough hours for their work. So, it can be concluded that Committees are quite influential in affecting the Government if one measures it in terms of time spent by them for their work. (Sanyal, 2011)

A qualitative study in this regard would be relatively subjective. One can include quality of discussions; the innovations in the procedures of Parliament, the manner Committees conduct their business, etc., to assess the effectiveness of Parliamentary Committees in India. According to Subhash Kashyap, "The three financial Committees play a crucial role in the task of a detailed scrutiny of Governmental spending and performance, thereby securing the accountability of the administration to the Parliament in financial matters. The accountability of the administration to the Parliament is not direct and is exercised through Ministers, but in the Committees, the civil servants come face to face with Committees when they are called for oral evidences and are subjected to extensive examination. The relentless crusade of the Financial Committees to this end keeps the administration on its toes." (Kashyap, 2012)

He further adds that Action Taken Report is essentially an Indian innovation for follow- up of the recommendations(Kashyap, 2012).

While measuring the effectiveness of the Parliamentary Committees in India, it is important to note that these Committees are instruments of Parliament, not of Government. Their role is of great significance, yet advisory only. Since India is a Parliamentary Democracy, legislative process here is led by the Executive itself. Keeping this in mind, we have to recognize the limits also of these Committees in influencing the whole Legislative process.

Shortcomings of Committee System in India

In 2002, National Commission to Review the Working of the Constitution (NCRWC) conducted a study on Committee System in India and it pointed out some shortcomings of Committees in India, which are as follows:

- Low attendance of MPs at meetings,
- Too many ministries under a Committee,
- Norms not followed by most political parties while nominating MPs to Committees,
- The Constitution of DRSCs for a year leaves very little time for specialisations.

NCRWC recommended some reforms also which are mentioned as below:

- DRSCs should be periodically reviewed. All bills should be referred to DRSCs. They must be enabled to elicit public views and call experts' advice.
- Three nodal Committees should be set up as the first one on the National Economy (to provide analysis of the National Economy), the second one on the Constitution (to scrutinise Constitutional Amendment Bills before they are introduced in Parliament) and the third Committee on Legislations (to oversee and coordinate legislative planning). In the words of M. P. Singh and Rekha Saxena, this suggestion of NCRWC is the 'most out of the box' suggestion for restructuring the Parliamentary Committee system in India as it would enable continuity and specialisation in Committee's work which will be independent from Government interference. These committees would be able to work in coordination with the Cabinet Committees without duplication.
- NCWRC also suggested for smaller size and longer tenure for committees. (Singh & Saxena, 2012).

Committee System in other Countries

Most of the democracies in today's world have Committee system as it is neither possible nor expected from members of Legislature to perform all kinds of works of a legislature which includes: scrutiny of the Bill; examination of Facts; regulation of Governmental activities, and most importantly, having expertise regarding financial matters. A comprehensive comparative study is neither possible here, nor desired, yet it would be helpful to have a glance on the committee system of a few countries India is closely connected with.

Committee System in UK

British parliament is called mother of all parliaments. Indian Parliamentary System, as we have discussed earlier, has lot many similarities with this system. Though British parliament is a soverign institution in theory, yet due to Prime-Ministerial System, decline in its powers is a concern. In the wake of decline of Parliamentary powers, Committees are assuming greater role here also. In the Parliament of the UK two kinds of Committees are found (1) Select Committees (2) Standing Committees

Select Committees

These Committees are formed either to scrutinise the work of Government or to suggest some measures on specific policy areas, like health, education, etc. These Committees are not permanent in nature and their term gets over with the completion of their task.

Standing Committees

These Committees are now named as individual Bills Committees. Generally, Standing Committees are permanent in nature; however, in the UK these Committees are dissolved with their recommendation on the Bill for which they are formed. That is why members of Committees do not get the kind of knowledge which members in countries like India and the USA do.

In general, though the Committees in the UK are also assuming greater responsibilities than ever before, they are weak in terms of their powers to influence legislation.

Committee System in USA

Woodrow Wilson once wrote about importance of Committee System in American Government, "it is not far from the truth to say that Congress in session is Congress on public exhibition, whilst Congress in its committee rooms is Congress at work." (Wilson, 1885). The USA's constitution is the oldest written constitution of the world with Presidential form of Government. Committees in USA have assumed greater powers to influence legislation with the growing responsibilities of Senate particularly.

In USA three kinds of Committees are found:

- **Standing Committees**

  These Committees are permanent in nature. These Committees hold the key of the most of the legislative work and scrutiny regarding financial matters in the USA. Since the USA is a Presidential system, Executive is not present in the Legislature there; these Committees have become quite autonomous. According to an American scholar, George B. Galloway, this growing autonomy of Committees in USA has rather interfered with the adoption of a coherent legislative programme. (Galloway, 1961).

- **Select/Special Committees**

  These Committees can be permanent as well as *ad-hoc* in nature and are formed with separate resolution of the chamber for some investigation or some particular purpose of scrutiny.

- **Joint Committees**

  These Committees are consisted of members from both the chambers. These Committees are permanent in nature but they normally perform housekeeping business and may conduct inquiries if they are referred to do so. These Committees normally do not suggest measures as far as legislative work is concerned.

Committee System in Canada

Committee System in Canada also is an outcome of the need to perform those functions which cannot be adequately performed by Parliament. Like any other country, committee system has undergone reformative process here. Committees in Canada can be broadly categorized into three categories.

1. Committee of the Whole House

   Chaired by the Deputy Speaker, this committee includes all members of the HOUSE OF COMMONS meeting in its normal chamber. Until 1969 the Commons used to meet as a Committee of the Whole house to consider legislation clause by clause after second reading of a bill, a task now delegated to the relevant standing Committee. Estimates were also considered in Committee of Supply, and many members would like some estimates to be considered there again, because Committee of the Whole House is a public forum attracting great media attention. The Committee of Ways and Means, another version of Committee of the Whole House, which dealt with revenue, is now purely symbolic.

2. Standing Committees

   Standing Committees in Canada also occupy a place of prominence. The standing committees are the essence of the present committee system and they have three distinct functions which may be described as legislative, financial and investigative.

   Much of the detailed work of the House of Commons is carried out by committees. At one time all bills were referred to committee of the whole House, but since the reform of the standing committee system in 1968, most of them are now referred to standing committees.. These Committees generally perform their subject specific work. Their work normally includes investigation of financial matters, and scrutiny of legislation. There are joint standing committees also, consisting of members from both the houses. These joint committees perform scrutiny of the delegated legislative work, i.e. legislation by executive by authority of an Act of Parliament.

   Bills, waiting to become Acts, the estimates of government departments and subjects of inquiry are referred to the standing committees in accordance with their various subject areas. In dealing with bills and estimates, the standing committees remove a great deal of detailed work from the floor of the House. In undertaking special investigations they pursue their more traditional function of inquiry. Standing committees are empowered to call witnesses and appoint sub-committees. Standing Committee there can travel and hire specialists also for expert advice by authority of the House. They have to submit their reports to the House which are of advisory nature only, and it is always up to the will of the House to follow them. Standing Committees are also sometimes alleged to be partisan in nature and government controlled

But that does not mean that committees are ineffective in terms of their power of influence. Control of public finance is one such area where Public Accounts Committee exercises control in good measure. The special feature of this committee is that it is always, by convention, chaired by member of opposition. This committee is assisted by Auditor General in this task. Even if the report of a committee is advisory in nature, it helps in publicizing the existing discrepancies, if any, by drawing the attention of the House.

Such control over finances as the House is now able to exercise is due to the committee system to a large extent. The Standing Committees have the opportunity of scrutinizing the details of proposed departmental spending and reporting to the House before the money is voted. The Standing Committee on Public Accounts, whose chairman is by custom a member of the opposition, has the special function of examining public expenditure after it has been incurred. In carrying out its investigation, it is assisted by the Auditor General who makes an annual report to the Parliament. The Committee examines witnesses from the departments of government and draws the attention of the House to any irregularities it might discover.

3. Special Committees

   These Committees are formed for a specific period and with a specific function. These committees are not permanent in nature. Sometimes they are formed to gauge public opinion regarding some decisions of the government. As they are assigned some special task, so, at times they are called as 'task force' also. Special committees are appointed on an ad hoc basis and consist of not more than 15 members.

Conclusion

With this comparative study regarding the role of Committees of legislatures, it can be concluded that Committees in India are neither so weak as they are in the UK Parliament, nor are they as autonomous as in the USA Congress. It can also be concluded here that committee system in India has some similarity with the Canadian Committee system. There is no doubt about this observation that the Committees in Indian Parliament have occupied a place of pride and they have been able to influence the legislative work for the betterment of the whole Indian Political System. Actually, the thrust of democracy, i.e., debate and discussion, that too in a non-partisan manner, can be achieved by committee system in a meaningful way. Reforms adopted in 1993 with the establishment of 17 DRSCs of Parliament, have been commended by NCWRC as 'A Path-Breaking Innovation,' yet there are caveats which also need to be focused upon. In future, recommendations of NCRWC can prove as a guide for such efforts in this direction.

Review Questions:

1. What do you understand by Parliamentary Committee? Discuss the evolution and growth of committee system in India.
2. Discuss the types of Parliamentary Committee with special focus on Department related Standing Committee.
3. Critically analyse the role of DRSCs influencing the legislative work and ensuring accountability of Executive towards Parliament. Discuss the areas of reforms .
4. Discuss the need and role played by Parliamentary Committees.
5. Write short notes on the following:
    a) Need of the Committee System
    b) Functions of Committee System
    c) Need of the reform in the Committee System

References:

1. Galloway, B. G., (1961). 'History of the House of representatives.' Thomas Y. Crowell, New York./https://www.revolvy.com/main/index.php?s=Congressional%20committee&item_type=topic/accessed on 18.2.17
2. http://www.thecanadianencyclopedia.ca/en/article/committees/ Accessed on 18.2.17
3. Kashyap, S, (2012). "Our Political System." National Book Trust, New Delhi.
4. Kaul, M. N., & Shakdhar, S. L. (2001). "Practice and Procedure of Parliament," edited by G. C. Malhotra, published by Lok Sabha Secretariat & Metropolitan Book Co. Pvt. Ltd.Malhotra, G. C., (2004). "Parliamentary Committees with Special Reference to Departmentally Related Standing Committees." Bureau of Parliamentary Studies and Training, Lok Sabha secretariat.
5. Sanyal, K.(2011) "Strengthening Parliamentary Committee", PRS Legislative Research,Centre for Policy Research,New Delhi. http://www.prsindia.org/parliamenttrack/discussion-papers/strengthening-parliamentary-committees-2788/ accessed on 18.2.2017.
6. Singh, M. P., & Saxena, R. (2010). "Indian Politics: Contemporary Issues and Concerns". PHI Learning Private Limited, New Delhi.
7. Tyagi, R. (2004). "Indian Government and Politics." Mayur Paperbacks, Noida.
8. Wilson, W. (1885). "Congressional Government," quoted in the JCOC final report, archieved on December 27, 2006, at the wayback machine.

Six

Budget and Budgetary Process in India

Dr. Moitri Dey

The term 'Budget' was derived from a French word 'bougette' which means a sack or pouch from which the Chancellor of Exechequer used to take out his papers, for laying before the Parliament containing Government's financial plan for the following year.

In India, 'Budget System' was introduced on 7th April,1860. James Wilson, who was the first Indian Finance Member delivered the budget speech expounding the Indian financial policy as an integral whole for the first time. After independence, the first budget was presented by India's first Finance Minister Sri R.K. Shanmugham Chetty on November 26, 1947(GoI, 2010). Independent India saw an array of reforms in the budgetary process primarily with the launch of a wide range of socio economic development through five-year plans divided into Annual Plans. With successive Finance Commissions, a sound system of sharing resources with the State was established. The present system which is in place has by and large evolved over a period of time.

The annual exercise of budgeting is a means for detailing the road map for efficient use of public resources. Although, the Indian Constitution does not mention the term 'Budget', Article 112 provides that the President shall in respect of every financial year cause to be laid before both the Houses of Parliament, the House of People (Lok Sabha) and the Council of States (Rajya Sabha), a statement of the estimated receipts and expenditure of the Government for that year. This statement known as the 'Annual Financial Statement' is the main fiscal or budgetary document of the Government.

The financial year for the Union and the State Governments in India is from 1st April to 31st March. Each financial year is, therefore, spread over two calendar years. The period of financial year as from 1st April to 31st March was introduced in India from 1867. Prior to that, the financial year in India used to commence on 1st May and ended on 30th April. L.K. Jha Committee was appointed in May,1984 to look into the issue of financial year. The Committee while recommending the commencement of financial year from January mainly with reference to the impact of South West monsoon on the economy, had mentioned in their Report that if for any reason, a changeover to the calendar year is not acceptable despite its many advantages, then on balance, it might be best to live with the existing financial year and avoid the problems of transition.(GoI, 1985).

Budget is an essential activity which is carried out both by the government as well as private administration. Neither a government nor a private organization can function without Budget. Let us look at some the definitions of Budget.

Harold R. Bruce:"A Budget is a financial statement, prepared in advance of the opening of a financial year, of the estimated revenue and proposed expenditures of a given organisation for the ensuing year."

Dimock and Dimock: "A budget is a financial plan and projecting it over a specified period of time in future."

William Franklin Willoughby: Budget is "an integral and indispensable tool of administration".

However, there is a difference in nature and scope of government budget and private budget making.

To understand the concept better let us look at some of the basic differences between government budget and private budget pointed out by M.M.Sury:

1. Individuals, unlike governments, may at their own risk, earn and spend without planning, foresight, and proper recording of their transactions. Government in democracies is answerable for their actions to the legislators who in turn enjoy the mandate of the electorate.

2. A private individual may prefer to keep his financial transactions a secret whereas financial activities of the government get wide publicity and are subject to audit and inspection.
3. Financial resources at the disposal of individuals are far less than those available to a government. Like a government, a private organisation cannot impose taxes nor can it print currency. However, this is not a limitation with the government.
4. An individual regards surplus budget as a virtue and a means to accumulate capital and become rich. Contrarily, deficit budgeting is more a rule than an exception for the government.
5. Private budgeting is guided exclusively by profit motive while public budgeting has social welfare as the objective function.

Harold D. Smith in his book, "The Management of Your Government" (1945) sets out eight budgetary principles to accomplish the above tasks. These are:

1. Executive Programming: Budget, being the programme of the Chief Executive, goes hand in hand with programming and consequently must be under the direct supervision of the Chief Executive.
2. Executive Responsibility: The Chief Executive must see that the departmental programme fulfill the intent of the legislature and due economy is observed in the execution of the programme.
3. Reporting: Budgetary process like preparation of estimates, legislative action and the budget execution must be based on full financial and operating reports coming from all levels of administration.
4. Adequate Tools: The Chief Executive must have an adequately equipped budget office attached to him, and an authority to earmark monthly or quarterly allotment of appropriations.
5. Multiple Procedures: The method of budgeting may vary according to the nature of operations. Thus, the budgeting of quasi-commercial activities may be different from that of purely administrative activities.

6. Executive Direction: Appropriations should be made for broadly defined functions of the department allowing, thereby, sufficient discretion to the executive to choose means of operation to realise the main purpose.
7. Flexibility in Timing: Budget should have provisions to accommodate necessary changes in the light of changing economic situation.
8. Two-Way Budget Organization: Efficient budgeting depends upon the active cooperation of all departments and their sub-divisions.

Significance of Budget

Budget is not only a financial tool but also a management tool that sets out programmes and projects for socio-economic development. It helps to establish the cost constraints for a project, program or operation. It also helps in coordinating the activities of the programmes or policies between various stakeholders. Further, it helps in controlling resources; strive to achieve the set budget goals, evaluating the performance of administrators, etc.

Government Budget have various significance and purpose which needs to be highlighted. They are:

1. It is through budget government tries to maintain a balance between scarce resources and limitless demands. It done at various stages of budget i.e. preparation of estimates and expenditure, formulation and implementation of budget.
2. Budget is also an instrument for administration. It includes all the activities of government departments, public corporations and government aided agencies. It provides financial guidelines to the administrators on how to carry out their work. It clarifies and defines the administrative roles and responsibility.
3. Budget is an important tool through which plans and public policies are put into action. It converts policies which are conceived in paper into concrete activities. It is also a way through which policies are constantly evaluated and in turn enhance their implementation.

4. Budget enables financial and legal accountability of the executive to the legislature. It also ensures that similar accountability on the part of each subordinate authority. There is a system of Audit which is undertaken to check the expenditure is incurred as per budgetary sanctions and as per the purpose sanctioned in the budget.
5. Budget is a large document which reflects the entire activities of the government and contains all the valuable information on all the ministries and departments. It is classified in a functional manner which gives a clear picture of the government's effort in each area. It also contains various economic indicators like national income, consumption, expenditure, capital investment, deficit financing, etc. which is significant information for business firms and industrialists. The citizens also get to know various activities of the government.
6. It provides information about overall performance and the performance of a particular policy. Performance data collected on a continuous basis which strengthens the data base for evaluating and reformulating the policies, priorities and programmes.

Types of Budget

There are various types of budget which are conceived and practiced in different countries.

1. Line-item budget: It is also called traditional or conventional budgeting. This budgetary system evolved in England during 18th and 19th century. It was viewed primarily as a legal and accounting instrument, and the budget agency had the main responsibility of consolidating money estimates of expenditure needs from the various departments each year. In this form of budget, the emphasis is on the item (object) of expenditure without highlighting the purpose. The budget is conceived in financial terms. In this system, the amount granted by the legislature on a specific item should be spent on that item only. A line-item budget shows how many clerks will be hired,how much travel money will be spent, how much will go for printing or mimeographing, and what will be expended for papers,typewriters and stationery. (Basu, 1994). The

purpose of this budgeting is to avoid wastages over spending and misuse of money granted by the legislature to the executive. It also ensures accountability of funds i.e. ensuring legality and regularity of expenditure.

There are demerits of this system of budgeting. It is difficult to find out the broad purpose and objective resources being allocated. It does not help the management to control and appraise the performance and execution of programmes. It does not permit proper analysis of government transactions and too much stress on accountability and economy may make the administration slow.

2. Performance budget: The term was first coined by Hoover Commission in 1949. The system has its origin in U.S.A. It is also known as functional budget. It is a financial document that seeks the implementation and control of government programmes through budget allocation. This is done by presenting government operations in terms of programmes, activities and functions. Through such a functional classification of governmental financial operations, public policies are sought to be identified in the annual budget in concrete physical terms so that a direct interaction between inputs and outputs could be identifiable cost overheads. In performance budget, the focus is on the end rather than the means. The main purpose is to clearly define the objects of governmental spending, the work to be performed and an estimated cost of the performance. It serves as a basis for efficiency and work measurement qualitatively and quantitatively.

   Performance budgeting was adopted on the recommendation of the Estimates Committee in its twentieth report. It reiterated this recommendation again in its report in 1960. Frank W. Krause was given the assignment to study the appropriateness and viability of this system of budgeting in India. Finally, in 1968, following the recommendation of the Administrative Reforms Commission, performance budgeting was adopted in four central ministries. Further many state governments and other departments also adopted the system. However, this budgeting system has limitation in India. In India since there is no universal norms and standards of performance evaluation much of the benefits of efficiency and performance are lost. There are regional diversities which have resulted in different local precedents in costing procedures. Never the less, if the shortcomings are overcome then the budget can increase efficiency, effectiveness, accountability and performance of all the programmes and policies.

3. Planning-Programming-Budgeting (PPB) : The concept of Planning-Programming Budgeting (PPB) was introduced in the U.S.A. This type of Budgeting was adopted by the General Motors, an American automobile company in 1924. In 1964 it was followed in the Department of Defence of the federal government which was a success. So, President Johnson prescribed it for the entire budget in 1965. PPB is the process of converting the goals, programmes and projects into money estimates for review within the administrative branch and final action by the legislation.
4. Zero based budget: Zero based budget originated in the U.S.A. This budget was shaped by Peter A. Pyhrr who was a manager in a private industry. The system was adopted in 1978 in the U.S.A. by the then President Jimmy Carter. In this budgeting system, every programmes and schemes should be critically reviewed and re evaluated from zero before being included in the budget. It means all the programmes have to restart from the base (zero) instead of adopting an incremental approach. It is well known that an overriding characteristic of governments has been to continue the government schemes and programmes without any review, even after they have lost their relevance and have become outdated. Compared to the United States, for example, India does not have a 'sunset' provision by which each scheme and programme comes to and end on a predetermined date. One way of doing so is to introduce the concept of zero based budgeting system. The advocates of zero based budgets regard it as pragmatic approach which offers an extremely flexible management tool. It can lead to substantial savings. Low priority programmes can be eliminated or reduced. Programme effectiveness can be dramatically improved, although it may or may not have a budgetary impact. High impact

programmes can obtain increased financial allocation by shifting resources within an agency and tax increases can be checked.

5. Gender budget: Gender budgeting means incorporating gender perspectives at various levels of budgeting. It is converting gender commitments into budgeting commitments. Through this budget, it tries to achieve gender mainstreaming so as to ensure that benefits of development reach women as much as women. It is not an accounting exercise but an ongoing process of keeping a gender perspective in policy formulation, its implementation and review. Gender budget entails dissection of the Government budgets to establish its gender differential impacts and to ensure that gender commitments are translated into budgetary commitment. The rationale for gender budgeting arises from recognition of the fact that national budgets impact men and women differently through the pattern of resource allocation. Women, constitute 48% of India's population, but they lag behind men on many social indicators like health, education, economic opportunities, etc. Hence, they warrant special attention due to their vulnerability and lack of access to resources. The way Government budgets allocate resources, has the potential to transform these gender inequalities. In view of this, Gender Budgeting, as a tool for achieving gender mainstreaming, has been propagated.(GoI, 2017).

   In 2004, the Finance Ministry mandated the setting up of gender budget cells in each ministries/ departments. So, far 56 ministries/ departments have set up gender cells. India formally adopted Gender Responsive Budgeting in 2005. The objective of Gender Responsive Budgeting is to create policies which are gender – neutral. It aims to integrate critical gender concerns into fiscal policies and administration to address disparities. Since 2005, every annual budget lists out two parts. There is Part A, which shows 'Women Specific Schemes', namely those which have 100 per cent allocation for women and Part B shows 'Pro Women Schemes', namely, where at least 30 per cent of the allocation is for women.

6. Green Budget: There have been increasing concern on the sustainability of environment. Hence, countries across the globe

are resorting to green budget in order to conserve the environment. Green budget is a tool devised to make programs and policies for conservation of environment. Green budget includes funding for policies to sustain natural resources like land, water, etc., meet environmental challenges, develop clean energy resources, etc. The purpose of green budget is to integrate the environmental factors with every aspect of the economy. Also, to see that natural resources are not misused.

Under article 112 of the Constitution of India, the President causes to be laid before the house of Parliament a statement of the estimated receipts and expenditures of the Government of India. The financial management of Indian government is governed by Articles 112 to 117 of the Indian Constitution. However, nowhere in the Indian constitution the term 'budget' is used. It is referred as Annual Financial Statement which is the basic budget document. It shows the sums charged on the Consolidated Fund of India and the money required for meeting other expenditures. The former is non-votable and the latter votable. Votable estimates are submitted to the Lok Sabha, which can assent to,refuse or reduce the grant but not enhance it. All demands for grants and taxation proposals thus emerge from the executive. Expenditure can be sanctioned only by the Parliament. It is not only a constitutional provision but is also essential for policy formulation and competent resource allocation. The annual final financial statement includes the actual receipts and expenditures of the government for three consecutive years.

The Annual Financial Statement shows the receipts and expenditure of Government in three separate parts under which Government accounts are maintained are discussed below:

1. Consolidated Fund of India: Under Article 266(1) of the Constitution of India, all revenues received by the Government of India, all loans raised by the Government by issue of treasury bills, loans or ways and means advances and all moneys received by the Government in repayment of loans shall form one consolidated fund to be titled the "Consolidated Fund of India". All expenditure of the government is incurred from this fund and no amount can be withdrawn from this fund without approval by the Parliament.

No money from this fun can be issued unless the expenditure is authorized by an Appropriation Act whether the expenditure is charged on the Consolidated Fund or it is an amount voted by the Lok Sabha. Under the Constitution, certain items of expenditure e.g. emoluments and allowances of the President, salaries and allowances of the Chairman and the Deputy Chairman of Rajya Sabha and Speaker and the Deputy speaker of Lok Sabha,salaries; allowances and pensions of the Judges of the Supreme Court and the Comptroller and Auditor general of India, interest on the repayment of loans raised by Government and the payments to satisfy decrees of courts, etc. are charged on the Consolidated Fund of India. The charged items are shown in the Annual Financial Statement.

The Consolidated Fund of India is divided into two Accounts i.e. Revenue account and Capital account. Revenue account deals with the proceeds of taxation and other receipts classed as Revenue and expenditure met there from. On the other hand, capital account deals with expenditure incurred with the purpose of either increasing the concrete assets of durable nature or of reducing recurring liabilities. It is logical otherwise to meet capital expenditure from borrowed funds, the liabilities in respect of which are spread over a number of years, as the benefits arising from Capital expenditure flow over a period of years. It also includes various types of capital receipts like receipt heads, expenditure heads, public debt and loans and advances.

2. Contingency Fund of India: As the name suggest, this is a fund used when there is an emergency and unexpected expenditure. Under Article 267 of the Constitution of India, a "Contingency Fund" may be established, by law, by Parliament into which shall be paid from time to time such sums as may be determined by such law, and the said fund shall be placed at the disposal of the President, to enable advances to be made by him out of such fund for the purposes of meeting unforeseen expenditure pending authorization of such expenditure by Parliament. It is an advance fund placed at the disposal of the President to meet urgent expenditure pending

authorization by Parliament. Parliamentary approval for such expenditure and for withdrawal of an corresponding amount from the Consolidated Fund of India is subsequently obtained and the amount spent from Contingency Fund is recouped to the Fund.

From the financial year 2005-06, the corpus of the Contingency Fund of India has been enhanced to Rs.500 crore. This was done under clause 115 of the (Finance) bill of 2005, by transfer of an additional amount of Rs 450 crore from the Consolidated Fund of India to the Contingency Fund of India. Out of this corpus of 500 crore, 5 crores is kept at the disposal of Ministry of Railways. The Central Government established its Contingency Fund under the Contingency Fund of India Act, 1950 and has also framed the 'Contingency Fund of India Rules' under Section 4 of that Act. The Contingency Fund of India can be enhanced through a Finance Bill when the House is in session or through Ordinance if the House is not in session, in case the situation so warrants. Withdrawal from the Contingency Fund of India takes place with the approval of Secretary, Department of Economic Affairs, in terms of the Contingency Fund of India Act, 1950. In Government accounts, Contingency Fund has a single Major Head to accommodate all transactions of the fund.

3. Public Accounts: Other then, the normal receipts and expenditures of the Government which relate to the Consolidated Fund, certain other transactions enter Government account – in respect of which Government acts more as a banker, for example, transactions relating to Provident Fund, small savings, collections, other deposits, etc. The funds thus received are kept in the Public Account and the connected disbursements are also made therefrom. In brief, all other public moneys received by or on behalf of the Government of India are credited to the Public Account of India as empowered vide Article 266(2) of the Constitution of India. Such funds, however, remain merged in the cash balance of the Central Government, (with the Reserve Bank of India as the bankers to the Government), till payments are made to those to whom the funds pertain or are utilized for general or specific purposes as in

the case of Reserve Funds, or necessary adjustments are made, for example in the case of inter-Government transactions. The net funds in the Public Account are also available for financing the expenditure of Government. The Public Account transactions are grouped according to sectors and sub-sectors which are further sub-divided into Major Heads of Account and further down as per the accounting classification system of Government.

Budget is an important exercise in modern times with the unprecedented increase in governmental expenditures. It provides principles, tools and techniques for financial management. In India, the agencies which are involved in the budgetary process are:

- **Executive:** They are one who needs and spends the funds. It is the administrative ministries who have detailed knowledge of administrative requirements.
- **Legislature:** They grant the funds and appropriate them to particular ministries and departments;
- **Finance Ministry:** It controls and coordinates the entire activities involved in formulation and implementation of budget. It provides the required leadership and direction to other agencies.
- **Planning Commission:** Planning Commission which has been renamed as Niti (National Institution for Transforming India) Ayog on 1st January, 2015. It act as the premier policy think tank of the Government of India. It provides directional and policy input to the government.
- **Audit:** Auditing is done by the Comptroller and Auditor General of India. They see whether the funds are spent in conformity. They provide accounting skills to all the agencies in formulating budget estimates.

The Budget which is presented in the Parliament comprises of general budget and railway budget, demand for grants, vote on account, supplementary demands for grants and excess demands for grants, appropriation bill and finance bill. The budget is presented to the Lok Sabha in two parts i.e. Railway budget and General budget. The railway budget pertains to Railway finance and General budget which gives an overall financial status of the government. The railway budget was separated in 1924 on the recommendation of Acworth Committee (1920-21). The idea behind this separation was to secure stability for civil estimates by providing for an assured contribution from railway revenues and also to introduce flexibility in the administration of the Railway finance. The railway budget is presented by the railway minister proceeding to the presentation of general budget by the Finance Minister. The railway budget has been merged to the general budget from the financial year 2016-17. The Finance Minister presented both railway budget as well as general budget. However, the functional autonomy of the railway budget will be maintained.

The budgetary process in India can be broadly divided into three phases i.e. preparation, legislation (enactment) and execution

Preparation of Budget

Budget preparation starts in September-October by the Finance Ministry. The Ministry sends forms and circulars to Administrative Ministries for their estimates of expenditure for the upcoming financial year. The forms includes actual figure of previous years, estimates of current year and proposed estimates for next year. The Administrative Ministry passes these forms to the Drawing Disburse Officer or designated budget office. Drawing disburse Officer means a head of office and also any other Gazetted Officer so designated by a Department of the Central Government, a Head of Department or an Administrator, to draw bills and make payments on behalf of the Central Government. The term shall also include a Head of Department or an Administrator where he himself discharges such function;(GoI, 2016).

The Head of the Department after receiving the estimates from the drawing officers scrutinize and consolidates them for the entire department and submits them to the administrative ministry. The Administrative Ministry also scrutinizes the estimates in light of its general policy and consolidates them for the whole ministry and submits them to the Finance Ministry.

The Finance Ministry on receiving the budget estimates from all the Administrative Ministries consolidates these estimates in January. They are next scrutinized by the accountant general. In case, there is any kind of conflict between the Finance Ministry and Administrative Ministry on the inclusion of a scheme in the budget estimates, the Administrative Ministry can submit such estimates to the Cabinet. However, the decision of the Cabinet shall be final. Further, the Finance Ministry consolidates the budget estimates expenditures. On the basis of the estimated expenditures, the Finance Ministry prepares the revenue estimates in consultation with Central Board of Direct Taxes and the Central Board of Indirect Taxes. The Income Tax Department, Central Excise and Customs Department also provide assistance to Finance Ministry. The Finance Minister and other officials from Finance Ministry meet with industry associations, NGOs, experts, economists and other stakeholders to understand their expectation from the budget. Once the budget is finalized by the Finance Ministry, it is placed before the cabinet for approval. The Finance Ministry provides a brief summary of the budget before presenting in the Lok Sabha. Till the time, budget is presented in the Lok Sabha, it is a confidential document and should not be leaked. Further, an authorization to present in the Parliament is sought from the President.

Legislation of the Budget

Budget is most important tool for legislative control over the public purse and through the purse over the executive. It includes control of revenue and expenditure. No tax can be collected without its prior authorization and no expenditure incurred without its prior approval. Earlier following the colonial tradition, the finance minister presents the budget towards the end of February. Breaking the tradition, the Union budget for 2017-18 was presented on the 1st February, 2017. The purpose is to advance it by a month so that the legislative approval for annual spending plans and tax proposals could be completed before the beginning of the new financial year i.e. 1st April.

Earlier, the budget was presented to the Parliament in two parts. One was railway budget which was presented by the Railway Minister and general budget by the Finance Minister. From the year 2017-18, the railway budget has been merged with the general budget. The Finance Minister presents the Budget with a speech known as 'Budget Speech'. It is much awaited by various sections of the people starting from a layman to industrialist. It gives a glimpse of what is in store for them in the budget. It is a lengthy document which explains at length the financial proposals of the government, overall spending of all the ministries/departments, new policies and schemes and revenue raising proposals. The printed copies of budget speech, budget estimates and explanatory memoranda are circulated among members of the Parliament. After the presentation of budget in Lok Sabha, the budget is laid before the Rajya Sabha which can only discuss and has no vote power.

Two to three days after the budget presentation are allotted for the parliamentarians to go through the budget. Then the general discussion on the budget starts. However, the details of the budget are not discussed, only the general principle and policy underlying the budget are discussed. During discussion no voting or cut motions are allowed. The objective is that the members of the House have an opportunity to discuss revenue estimated, the ways and means programme of the Government and the 'charged' expenditure. The discussion has to be limited to the point whether the items of expenditure ought to be increased or decreased having regard to the importance of a particular item and also to the manner in which the Budget is framed. It is also an indication of the House on budget proposals for taxes as well as expenditure. At the end of the debate, the Finance Minister gives a general reply to the various charges made by the members. Grievances which have no relation to the points raised in the finance's Minister's speech or do not directly arise out of the proposed expenditure are not in order at this stage. Specific points or grievances and details of taxation and expenditure are addressed when the Demands for Grants and the Finance Bill are before the House.

After the presentation of the budget, the introduction of the finance bill and demands for grants has to be passed before the financial comes to an end i.e.31st March. General budget has 109 demands (103 civil and 6 defence) and railways has 32 demands. The demands for grants are voted on the basis of the priority of demands previously agreed to by the leaders. The Ministry of Parliamentary Affairs holds a meeting of the leaders of parties/groups in Lok Sabha after the presentation of the Budget for selecting and order of discussion on demands for grants of the ministries which are to be discussed in the House and the time to be allotted. Once it is decided, government forwards the proposals for the consideration of the Business Advisory Committee. The Committee after receiving the proposal from the government submits the report to the House. On the basis of the acceptance of the report submitted by the Committee, the allocation of time to various Ministries whose Demands for grants are to be discussed in the House is published in Bulletin Part-II. The Minister of Parliamentary Affairs after consulting the programme and convenience of the Ministers concerned prepares a time table showing the dates on which the Demands of the various ministries would be taken up in the House and forwards the same to Lok Sabha Secretariat. This is also published in Bulletin Part-II for the information of Members and Ministries. The demands for grants are deemed to have been moved and proposed from the Chair so the concerned minister need not formally move the demands for grants. The Minister, may if he so likes, initiate discussion on the Demands for Grants relating to his Ministry.

Only the votable items are put to vote while non-votable items like emolument of President, Speaker, Deputy Speaker, Judges of Supreme Court, Comptroller and Auditor General and Chairman of Union Public Service Commission are not put for voting. The non-votable items are also known as the 'charged expenditure'. The total number of days allotted for the voting of demands is 26 days. The Speaker, in consultation with the leader of the House, fixes a time limit for each demand as well as for the entire expenditure part of the budget. A demand is subjected to vote as soon as the time limit fixed for it, is reached. On the last day of the allotted period, the Speaker puts all the remaining demands to vote whether the discussion on the demand is complete or not. This process is known as Guillotine. It is a way to bring the financial proposals and debate to an end within a specified time. Consequently, outstanding demands have to be voted by the house without discussion.

During this stage, Member of Parliament can also move motions to reduce demands. Such motions are known as 'Cut Motions'. It is further divided into three categories:

1. Disapproval of Policy Cut: The form of such a cut motion representing disapproval of policy underlying a demand. The motion is to reduce the demand to Rs.1.
2. Economy Cut: It is to stress the likelihood of effecting economy in the proposed expenditure. This cut is used to reduce the proposed expenditure by a specified amount.
3. Token Cut: It is used generally by opposition to vent their grievances with the government of India. The motion is to reduce the demand by Rs.100. Through this motion, the lapses of administration are exposed. However, such motions are defeated because of the majority behind the Cabinet. A demand becomes a grant after it has been duly voted.

The Speaker decides whether a cut motion is or not admissible and may disallow any cut motion when in his opinion it is an abuse of the right of moving cut motions or is calculated to obstruct or prejudicially affect the procedure of the house, or is in contravention of the Rules of Procedure of the House.

Vote on Account: The process beginning with the presentation of the budget and ending with discussion and voting on demands for grants required sufficiently long time, a provision has been made in the Constitution which empowers Lok Sabha to make any grants in advance in respect of the estimated expenditure for a part of any financial year pending the completion of the procedure for the voting of the Demands for grants and passing of the Appropriation Bill. It is known as Vote on Account. The procedure regarding the Vote on Account was introduced for the first time in Lok Sabha in the Budget session, 1951. The period covered by vote on account is generally two months and the amount is approximately one-sixth of total demands.

Appropriation Bill: As per the Constitution, no money shall be withdrawn from the Consolidated Fund of India except under appropriation made by law. The voting on demands for grants by Lok Sabha does not by itself authorize the issue of money out of the Consolidated Fund of India to meet the grants. The Act is the only legal authority for the appropriation of money from the Consolidated Fund of India to meet the grants made by Lok Sabha and expenditure charged on the Consolidated Fund of India. Either of the Houses cannot make any amendment in the proposed Appropriation Bill. Any debate on the bill is limited to matters of public importance or administrative policy implied in the grants covered by the Bill which have not already been raised while the relevant demands for grants were under discussion. The Bill becomes an Act after getting the President's assent. Once it becomes an Act, government can withdraw money from the Consolidated Fund of India.

Finance Bill: Article 265 of the Constitution lies down that no tax shall be levied or. collected except by authority of law. Since Parliament is the law-making body, it is this august body which must give consent to the taxation proposals of the Government. Finance Bill is the bill embodying the government's financial(taxation) proposals for the ensuing financial year which has to be passed by the Parliament. It is open to general and clause discussion. Amendments may propose the abolition or the reduction of any tax but not any new tax nor an increase in the rate of any existing tax. The Bill as amended is passed by the Lok Sabha and after consideration by the Rajya Sabha. Then it goes to the President for his signature on receipt of which it becomes an Act.

Money Bill: Money Bill is one which is dealing with taxation, borrowing, or expenditure. There is a difference between Finance Bill and Money Bill in the following ways

- A money bill deals exclusively with taxation, borrowing, or expenditure whereas Finance Bill has a broader coverage in the sense that it deals with other matters as well.
- A Money Bill is a bill certified to be such by the Speaker of the Lok Sabha whereas Finance Bill requires no such certificate.
- A Money Bill must be returned by the Rajya Sabha to Lok Sabha within 14 days of receipt, with its recommendations, if any, which the Lok Sabha is not bound to accept. Disagreement over a Finance Bill, however, is resolved at a joint sitting by a majority of the total number of the members present and voting.

With the passage of Appropriation Bill and Finance, the budget is ready for execution. There is also a provision for supplementary grants.

After the Appropriation Act is passed, if it is found that the amount authorized is not sufficient for any functions or if a new activity arises or the expenditure incurred for execution of functions exceeds the amount passed through the budget, the President is authorized to lay before the Parliament a supplementary financial statement under Article 115 for supplementary grants. However, it is passed following the usual procedure followed for the passage of the Appropriation Act..

Execution

After the Appropriation Act is passed, the grants as voted by the Parliament are distributed, care being taken to spread the cuts, if any over numerous heads. Appropriation is the allocation of funds to a given unit as passed by Parliament. Within a grant, an intra-unit transfer of funds is permissible. Unspent balance, if any gets lapsed. Actual expenditure depends on two conditions i.e. sanction by competent authority and provision of adequate funds. The spending authority shall exercise due care in the spending of public money. Public money shall not be spent for the benefit of a particular individual or community. Execution of budget also involves: collection of revenue, custody of the collected funds and distribution of funds.

The Indian economy is federal in structure. The executive authority is exercised through the union government at the Centre as well as various state governments in accordance with the distribution of power given in the Constitution. Like, imposing a tax on income is sole domain of Central government. Similarly, state government has exclusive power to impose tax on the sale of commodities. The division of powers of taxation implies, amongst other things, that the Constitution visualized state intervention in the economy as a combined responsibility of the central and the state governments.

In a parliamentary democracy, four organs of the government exercise financial control in a parliamentary democracy. Parliament exercises control over revenue, expenditure, borrowing and accounts. Parliament through various committees keeps a control on the financial spending of various administrative agencies. The Finance Ministry has a vital responsibility in executing the budget. It has to ensure that the Administrative Ministries get adequate funds, which they keep within their grants, that they surrender their savings before the end of financial year, that they send regular progress report on their spending. It coordinates the activities of various departments/ministries, reviews the results and monitors the general trend of expenditure of the government. The Reserve Bank of India controls all the monetary aspects of the Indian economy. It is the head of the banking system, guiding and controlling the commercial banks as the custodian of state's monetary policy.

Accounting and Auditing

Accounting and Auditing is an important way to keep financial control by the Parliament. It ensures that the provisions of the budget passed by the Parliament are followed or not. It is the responsibility of the Comptroller and Auditor-General of India to control audits of both the Centre as well as State. Articles 148 to 151 of the Indian Constitution give the provisions for audit. It is also the responsibility of the Comptroller and Auditor-General of India to keep accounts of the Union (except the Railway and Defence Accounts) as well as the State. Until 1976, the maintenance of accounts and audit had remained combined in the hands of the Comptroller and Auditor-General. In 1976, the Central government separated accounting from audit. Since then, the Comptroller and Auditor-General has been entrusted with the responsibility of auditing only. A Controller-General has been appointed in the Central Government to be the technical authority heading the new accounting system. There is an Office of Accountant- General in each state to keeps the accounts of transactions in each state. However, the Comptroller and Auditor-General of India provide necessary skills, direction and guidelines for maintaining accounts. The state Auditor- General coordinates with treasuries in the state to maintain the expenditures and financial controls. The accounts of Railways are kept by the Financial Commissioner for Railways, and Defence by the Finance Ministry through the Financial Adviser (Defence) and the Military Accountant-General. Therefore, Comptroller and Auditor-General of India concentrate mainly on enduring conformity to rules and regulation and very rarely to performance audit.

Conclusion

Budget is the cornerstone of financial administration and the various operations in the field of public finance are correlated through the instrument of budget. Budget is the financial planning of an organization which reflects the revenues and expenditure of the organization. A government budget is a financial statement which consists of the revenues and expenses passed by the Parliament to be implemented in the upcoming financial year. A government ensures optimal allocation of scarce resources taking into account larger socio economic condition of the country. Therefore, budgeting involves determining for a future time period on what is to be done and achieved, the manner in which it is to be done and the resources required for the same.

Review Questions:

1. What do you mean by Budget?
2. What are the types of Budget?
3. What is the significance of Budget?
4. Briefly explain the legislation of budget in India.
5. Do you think Budget is an important tool for financial control in India?

References:

1. Basu, Rumki, (2004) "Public Administration: Concepts and Theories" (5th Edition), Sterling Publishers Private Limited, New Delhi
2. Bruce, Harold R., (1952) "American National Government", Henry Holt and Company.
3. Dimock, Marshall E and Gladys Ogden Dimock (1983) "Public Administration", Holt McDougal,5th edition.
4. Government of India(1985) "L.K.Jha Committee's Report on Change in Financial Year", Government of India
5. Government of India (2004) "Budget in Parliament", Bureau of Parliamentary Studies and Training, Lok Sabha Secretariat, New Delhi.

6. Government of India(2010) "Budget Manual", Ministry of Finance, Government of India
7. Government of India(2016) "General Financial Rule", Ministry of Finance, Government of India.
8. Government of India(2017) "Budgeting for Gender Equity", Ministry of Women and Child Development, Available at http://wcd.nic.in/gender-budgeting, accessed on 28/1/2017.
9. Smith, Harold D., (1945) "The Management of Your Government", McGraw-Hill, Whittlesy House, New York
10. Sury, M.M., (2011) "Budgets and Budgetary Procedures in India: 1947-48 to 2009-10",
11. Willoughby, William Franklin, (1927) "The National Budget System, With Suggestions for its Improvement", The Johns Hopkin Press, University of California.

Seven

Role of Media in a Democracy

Dr. Simer Preet Kaur

Media can be defined as a communication channel which relays all types of information, like news, entertainment, education, data, or advertisements. The word comes from Latin plural of the word 'medium'.It includes different mediums like newspapers, magazines, T.V., radio, billboards, telephone, internet etc. Media can also be described as means or channels of universal communication in a society, playing a considerable role in keeping the masses updated about all the events in the world.

Media plays an important role in our polity and society. It gives us vast knowledge, and conveys information about various subjects. It updates information frequently to spread awareness amongst the general public, thus, raising the awareness of the masses. It provides facts, and figures for our analysis and proper understanding of important subjects. Media also plays a beneficial role for the society by raising social issues, and helps the voice of masses to reach the concerned authorities. It provides live or recorded telecast for various **events** helping people to see the true picture whether of a sports tournament or a political rally or speeches of our leaders. In a developing and democratic country, like India the media should neither be an adversary nor a collaborator with the government, rather it should play the role of a constructive critic.

Types of Media

There are many different types of media available in the modern world.

Broadly, there can be two main divisions of media, the print media such as Newspapers & Magazines and the electronic media such as Radio, Television, and the Internet. The media culture in India has evolved over centuries. It is a complex communications network that upholds the world's largest democracy. The media does not and cannot work in a vacuum; it reflects and is a product of a social environment which is a result of its historical complexities. The development of media in India has been loaded with difficulties; it had to struggle with colonial constraints, poverty, illiteracy, and apathy from the very beginning. Within this framework, it is imperative that media development in India should be divided into two broad periods: the colonial times, and post-independence press.

Newspapers

In India, newspaper history is inextricably linked with its political history. The first printing press was established in Bombay in 1674 followed by Madras in 1772. The first Indian newspaper was established in January 1780 and was named Calcutta General Advertise. It was Started by an Englishman called James Augustus Hickey, and so was also known as the Hickey's Bengal Gazette. Soon after that many other newspapers started like the Calcutta Gazette, the Bengal Journal, the Oriental Magazine, the Madras Courier and the Indian Gazette. After that the 19th century saw the birth of many English, Hindi and regional language newspapers.

These early newspapers were very important as they laid the foundation stone of Indian press which gained vibrancy and strength to reach the masses. With the rise of nationalism in India, newspapers which were a vehicle of information diffusion became an important instrument for freedom struggle. The first Hindi daily, called 'Samachar Sudha Varshan', began in 1854. Raja Ram Mohun Roy published a Bengali weekly called 'Sangbad Kaumudi', and a bi-lingual monthly called, 'Brahminical Magazine' in 1821. End of the 19th century saw the birth of many newspapers by eminent personalities like Rabindranath Tagore's Bengali newspaper called 'Sadhna', Madan Mohan Malviya's 'Abhyuday' etc. English language newspapers also arose, which became important mediums of information for the urban middle class India like the 'Statesman' from Calcutte, 'Times of India' in Bombay, 'The Mail' in Madras, and 'The Civil and Military Gazette' in Lahore. The first newspaper wholly owned by Indians, which became one of the finest newspapers in the world was 'The Hindoo Patriot' of Calcutta edited by Harish Chandra Mukherjee.

These Indian newspapers were very often critical of the British policies and used harsh term against them in their editorials. As the national struggle for freedom gained strength, there was an increase in the Indian newspapers. Along with newspapers, news agencies also started developing in India. In 1927, T. Sadanand started the 'Free Press of India Service'. After that V. Sengupta started 'United Press of India' in 1937.

During the national struggle for independence, newspapers became the chief device for carrying out political tasks like political propaganda, education of the masses, spreading of nationalist ideology consolidate nationalist public opinion. The Indian National Congress (INC) also propagated it's ideology through the Press. Many of the founding members of the INC in 1885 were journalists, and most of the major political leaders in India either owned a newspaper or contributed in them by their writings. Newspapers played the important role of effective opposition for the British Government.

At the time of independence in 1947, India had a dynamic and vibrant press culture. The press became truly free and unshackled from the restraints of the British rule. With technological developments and overall higher literacy level and increasing per capita income, the number of newspapers and their circulation has increased manifold. According to the registrar of newspapers of India, under the ministry of information and broadcasting, by the year 2013-14, there are a total of 99660 newspapers and periodicals published all over India. These include English, Hindi, as well as regional language publications.

With time media, especially big national dailies are mostly owned by the corporate houses, in race with each other to make bigger and bigger profits like commercial enterprises. After adopting LPG (Liberalization, Privatization, and Globalization) in 1991, the media industry welcomed foreign partnerships which increased its impact on masses.

Radio

Radio started in India with the first ever broadcast by the Radio Club of Bombay in June 1923. Three years later, in 1926 the Indian Broadcasting Company (IBC) was permitted to set up two stations at Bombay and Calcutta, both of which started the next year in 1927. The IBC liquidated in less than three years, and in April 1930, the Indian state Broadcasting Service, was started by the government. In 1936, Delhi radio station became functional, and in the same year the Indian State Broadcasting Service became All India Radio.

At the eve of independence, there were six radio stations in India, at Delhi, Bombay, Calcutta, Madras, Tiruchirapalli and Lucknow. In 1956 the national broadcasting service adopted the name Akashvani, and in 1957 a separate channel for popular film music was launched called Vividh Bharati.

The All India Radio is one of the largest media organizations in the world, with 105 regional stations, 65 local stations, and three Vividh Bharti broadcasting centres. It broadcasts in 23 languages and 146 dialects catering to the culturally diverse population of India. AIR also operate 18 FM radio channels, specially targeting the urban audience

In India, the medium of radio was intended to provide support to the procedure of socio-economic development. Radio, as a medium of communication proved to be more effective as compared to the print media. Radio reaches even those people who cannot read and educates even as it entertains. Modern technology has made mass media easily accessible to the masses, and it makes quicker and longer lasting impact on the people.

Television

Television broadcasts started in India under the aegis of All India Radio (AIR) on 15th September 1959 in Delhi. In the beginning there were only two programmes a week, with one hour duration of each. These were mainly educational programmes for children and farmers. By 1965, a daily one-hour service with a news bulletin was started, and service was extended to Mumbai in 1972. Television further extended its reach when in 1975 new television stations were started in Calcutta, Chennai,

Srinagar, Amritsar and Lucknow. Till 1975, only seven cities were covered by Doordarshan and it was the only T.V. channel in India.

In 1975-76 the government started a programme called Satellite Instructional Television Experiment (SITE) through which television programmes were made available in 2400 villages in the remote and least developed areas through a satellite. 1976 was an important year for T.V, when television services were separated from Radio. Doordarshan (DD) became a national channel, when it started telecasting national programmes 1982.

Colour TVs were introduced in India with coloured live telecast of the Independence Day parade on 15th August, 1982. The 1990's brought about a revolution in television history by the arrival of cable TV. These privately owned channels were powered by commercials, and latest technology, thus providing quality entertainment. Direct to Home (DTH) is now providing even better services to the mass of India.

Freedom of information through the mediums of press, radio and the TV is essential a thriving society and culture. Especially in developing countries grappling with problems of illiteracy and poverty the medium of television has the potential to reshape its political and social culture. TV channels, both from within the country and from abroad help to educate and update the masses of people.

Internet and Social media

The internet and various forums related to it like the social media, online newspapers, e-mail etc. have revolutionized the way we live and the way we interact. They are also sometimes called alternative media. It has also become one of the easiest and fastest medium of getting information and entertainment. In India, internet began with the launch of the Educational Research Network (ERNET) in 1986. Its main purpose was to provide help to educational and research organizations, and was not available for general public. On 14 August 1995, state-owned Videsh Sanchar Nigam Limited (VSNL) became the first internet service provider for general public.

This internet service was known as the Gateway Internet Access Service (GIAS), and was available in Mumbai, Delhi, Kolkata, Chennai,

Pune and Bangalore. The VSNL's internet service got 10,000 subscribers within the first 6 months of the launch. Broadband internet in India began in the year 2004, and in 2010, the government auctioned 3G spectrum followed by the auction of 4G spectrum that increased the speed of the wireless broadband.

The National e-Governance Plan (NeGP), states that "all information covering non-strategic areas [is placed] in the public domain to enable citizens to challenge the data and engage directly in governance reform." This clearly shows that the right to information is a part of the e-governance plan. This empowers the people to get governance information in the digital form as it is not possible to carry out this requirement through traditional paper-based processes. Accessing information is a basic human right and the internet is helping in securing it. Social media platforms like Facebook and Twitter can also become powerful tools to spread awareness about the right to information.

Role of Media in a Democracy

The primary role of media is to educate the society. Media exposes social and political issues and ignites peoples' awareness and education. It can also educate people about their rights and duties. Media is often called the fourth pillar of democracy along with legislature, executive and judiciary. Media plays an essential role in creating a democratic socio-political culture in the society. It supplies information, which helps citizens in assessing any given situation and base their decisions on. They spot problems in our society and polity, thus serving as a medium for deliberation. Media can also be called as watchdogs of those in power. Mass media can also become a public forum reflecting diversity in society, thus promoting harmony. The role of media in a democracy is a crucial one as they perform the important function of being intermediaries between the government and the masses.

The role of Media in democracy is as big and important as that of politicians. Democracy becomes meaningless if media is not free, neutral, vigilant, and active. This role of media can vary drastically depending on different things; much depends on the nature of the medium concerned, or on the state of democracy in a country, and also on the level of development in any given country. The foremost role of the media is to present information to the public, and to scrutinize on all the various socio-economic-political events in a country. The popularity of media is increasing among the masses and it influences the thoughts/opinions of its readers/viewers to a large extent. An impartial and neutral media acts as a watchdog of a democracy and a driving force behind good governance and transparency. It should desist from airing views which can adversely affect the political and social fabric of a country. It can assume an advocacy role, and report on what should be happening, rather than what is happening.

The role of media assumes even greater importance in developing countries where socio-political development is still underway. People with improved and enhanced information are greatly empowered to make better choices. According to James D. Wolfensohn, the president of the World Bank group, "A key ingredient of an effective development strategy is knowledge transmission and enhanced transparency. To reduce poverty, we must liberate access to information and improve the quality of information. People with more information are empowered to make better choices. For these reasons I have long argued that a free press is not a luxury. It is at the core of equitable development. The media can expose corruption. They can keep a check on public policy by throwing a spotlight on government action. They let people voice diverse opinions on governance and reform and help build public consensus to bring about change" (Islam, 2002) Media acts as a mechanism through which both democracy and development can flourish.

The media plays a positive role in a democracy when it is facilitated by a supportive and free environment. Freedom of media can be guaranteed by press laws and no government censure. Media can thrive and play a positive role only when media organizations are financially independent, is free from any form of state intervention or pressures, and has a competitive environment.

On the other hand, if media is biased, corrupt and partial, it can have disastrous effects on the functioning of democracy. Another factor is that media is focusing more and more on Entertainment as its main component, which has become a hindrance in its primary function which is to inform and educate people. "Mass media in established democracies mostly operate according to market principles, they disregard their democratic duties. This is alleged to have serious repercussions for democracy, causing apathy, cynicism and ignorance with regard to politics among citizens."

One of the strongest points of the media is the ability to bring about change, both in society and politics. Countries where media performs its role effectively will result in higher levels of political participation as well as higher accountability of elected representatives. "A better availability of information induces people to express their opinions at the polls and on the streets." (Müller, 2014). This clearly shows that an independent and vigilant media not only supports political and social development, but can bring about changes in a country's society and polity.

Freedom of Speech and Expression

The Indian Constitution guarantees the Freedom of speech and expression as a fundamental right subject to reasonable restrictions. Article 19(1) (a) of Indian Constitution stipulates that all citizens have the right to freedom of speech and expression. This right is subject to limitations imposed under Article 19(2) of the Indian constitution. It gives the citizens the right to express their convictions and opinions freely by words of mouth, writing, printing, pictures or any other mode. "Democracy – which recognizes that people have the right to elect a government of their choice – cannot exist in any meaningful way without the right to freedom of expression. There are many aspects to this rationale, but the fundamental concept is that in order for democracy to be effective, the citizenry that votes in elections and engages in public processes with government must be informed and must have the right to participate freely in public discourse." ('Workshop on Parliament and Media: Rajya Sabha)

The freedom of press or media, which has been fundamental in the evolution of the Indian society and polity, is intrinsic in the freedom of speech and expression. Freedom of press is essential for socio-political liberty and proper functioning of democracy. The media plays a very important role in our society and polity. It not just disseminates information but also helps form opinions in a society resulting in a healthy democracy.

Right to Information (RTI)

Right of speech and expression is further strengthened by the Right to information. The right to know, to receive and to communicate information is essential for the right to freedom of speech and expression to be absolute. It further helps in making the political system more responsive, accountable and citizen-friendly.

In the case of Raj Narain vs State of UP, in 1976, the Supreme Court had said that people cannot speak or express themselves unless they know. It further stated that in a democracy, People have a right to know how the government, which represents them, are functioning. That is why the right to know is a part of freedom of speech and expression.

Right to Information Act 2005 allows every citizen to: 1) Ask any questions from the Government, 2) seek out any information from the Government, 3) Take copies of and inspect any government documents or work, and 4) to take samples of materials of any Government work. This act covers the whole of India except the State of Jammu and Kashmir. All bodies, which are constituted under the Constitution or under any law or under any Government notification or all bodies, including NGOs, which are owned, controlled or financed by the Government are covered under this act.

Media Support in Legislative Procedures

Democracy is a government of the people, for the people and by the people, but this doesn't necessarily mean that people are active and actual partners in governance. A strong democracy cannot work effectively without active participation of its people. Media has the power to form a bridge which can shrink the gap between the government and its citizens. The most important function of any government is to legislate or to make laws for the country. Legislature lays down guidelines for executives for governing. They also have the authority to make or amend a country's laws.

Media does not have a defined or definite role in governance. It cannot change the decisions made by the government or the state. Nevertheless, the media plays a very important role in the functioning of a democratic society and polity. It gives voice to the citizens and communicates their opinion to the government. Access to governmental information is crucial for a democratic society as it ensures that citizens make responsible and informed choices. This access can be provided by media, only if they in turn get access to the process of legislation. The connection between legislators and the media is very complex. Media and legislators are mutually dependent on each other.

The media, through its power of shaping and influencing public opinion, can bring about changes to a law by reflecting a shift in people's opinions. It can cause public outrage or overwhelming interest about a particular issue or law, which in turn can pressurize the government to amend or make certain laws. Media provides public with information about how legislature works; it can draw attention to outdated and ineffective laws; it can point out loopholes in a law; or create awareness about need for certain laws, thus acting as a driving force for open communication between the legislature and general public.

For active participation and understanding of the legislative process, free and easy access to legislative procedures is a necessity. Both Parliament and Media are the voice of the people. It is imperative that both should work jointly in serving the people. Media not only needs easy access to parliament to get all the information, but also sufficient opportunities to know the nuances of reporting parliamentary matters. The parliament of India, comprising of the two houses use the power of media to empower the general public by giving free and easy access to the proceedings of Lok Sabha and Rajya Sabha live on their T.V.

Lok Sabha Television (LSTV)

Lok Sabha television is the Parliament Channel of India with the authorization to telecast live the proceedings of the Lok Sabha – the House of the People of Indian Parliament. It is a Public Broadcast channel displaying programmes related to legislation, governance, and socio-economic issues, legal and political matters.

It acts as a medium between viewers and the parliament of the country. The channel is devoted to bridge the gap between the people and their elected representatives by means of easy access to the work of legislative bodies of India. It is empowering the people of India by encouraging accountability and transparency in governance.

Rajya Sabha Television (RSTV)

Rajya Sabha TV showcases the upper house of the Indian Parliament. It telecasts live coverage of Rajya Sabha proceedings; provides comprehensive analysis of parliamentary affairs; discusses national and international affairs and present knowledge-based content for its viewers. Strengthening the relationship between Parliament and the people of India, the channel gives special attention to legislative business undertaken by the Parliament.

Both the houses of parliament give free and easy access to their proceedings, thus providing the citizens their fundamental right to access and information. Some of the state legislature assemblies are also making headway in this direction and providing the people with direct and uncensored proceedings of their legislatures. The Delhi assembly does not have a channel dedicated to showcasing its proceedings, but beams live webcast online of its assembly proceedings. The Assembly of Andhra Pradesh provides live feed to TV channels from inside the assembly, and Karnataka assembly also allows channels to record proceedings of the house.

However, most of the state assemblies do not disclose their assembly proceedings to the people or the media, thus obstructing public access to public information. Most of the states cite lack of funds as the main reason for not making the assembly proceedings public.

In 2012, PIL was filed in the madras high court by Lok Satta party of Tamil Nadu, demanding live telecast of the Tamil Nadu assembly. The PIL stated 'that people should not be left to watch and be influenced by partisan news channels that showed only conveniently packaged clips of the proceedings' (Plea for live telecast of Assembly proceedings: The Hindu) The proceedings of the house is recorded by cameras stationed in the house, and only edited footage is provided to the media and that to only on need to know basis. This means that the public generally remains unaware of the proceedings in the assembly.

Conclusion

A democratic system is incomplete without the active and voluntary participation of the masses, which cannot be done if the people are not informed about the various issues of legislature and governance. The role and importance of Media become very important components of a democratic society. Media can help in the efficient functioning of Parliament in many ways; it provides response from the people to the Parliament through voicing of public concerns and also provides information to the people so that they can appraise their chosen representatives and understand the workings of the Parliament and the Parliamentarians.

Review Questions:

1. What is the role of media in the law making process? Discuss with an example of print or electronic media.
2. Elaborate on the role of media in a democracy.
3. Write an essay on Right to Information Act.
4. Write about different types of media and their role in legislative process.
5. Write short notes on the following:
   a. Social Media
   b. Role of newspapers in a democracy
   c. Importance of media

References

1. Conservation India, (2015). "What is Right to Information and How To Use It?" http://www.conservationindia.org/wp-content/files_mf/What_is_Right_to_Information_and_how_to_use_it_final.pdfAccessed on 12/12/17
2. Government of India, (2017). https://data.gov.in/catalog/number-registered-newspapers-and-periodicals-language-all-india-and-state-wiseAccessed on 10/11/17
3. Government of India, (2009). 'Workshop on Parliament and Media'http://rajyasabha.nic.in/rsnew/press_media /04092009 .pdfAccessed on 05/11/17

4. http://pib.nic.in/newsite/erelcontent.aspx?relid=49043 Accessed on 24/12/17
5. Islam, Roumeen, (ed.) (2002). "The Right to Tell: The Role of Mass Media in Economic Development" The International Bank for Reconstruction and Development/World Bank, Washington, DC
6. London School of Economics and Political Science, (2014). "The Impact Of The Mass Media on The Quality of Democracy Within a State Remains a Much Overlooked Area Of Study".http://blogs.lse.ac.uk/eurocrisispress/2014/12/10/the-impact-of-the-mass-media-on-the-quality-of-democracy-within-a-state-remains-a-much-overlooked-area-of-study/ (Accessed on 28/11/17)
7. Müller, Lisa, (2014). "Comparing Mass Media in Established Democracies: Patterns of Media Performance" Palgrave Macmillan, UK
8. The Hindu, (2012). "Plea For Live Telecast of Assembly Proceedings" http://www.thehindu.com/news/national/tamil-nadu/plea-for-live-telecast-of-assembly-proceedings/article3529040.ece(Accessed on 22/09/17)

EIGHT

Role of Civil Society Organisation in Legislative Process

Ms. Paromita Datta

For defining and understanding various debates around the emergence and development of Civil Society Organisations, it is important to develop a comprehensive perception about Civil Society. The concept of civil society is complex. In general terms, it can be described as groups and associations which are not administered by the state or by its institutions. Civil society can be understood to be a political space where voluntary associations deliberately seek to shape the rules that govern aspects of social life. (Scholte, 2001). From the ancient Greek political thought till the emergence of liberal political thought in the 17th century, the concept of civil society was used to reflect state or political society. Classical political philosophers like Plato and Aristotle did not define the state and society in different terms. According to them, a person who is a member of the civil society is also a part of the state. It was with the advent of thinkers like Thomas Hobbes, John Locke in the 17th century that distinction between state and civil society started emerging. The modern conception of civil society as distinct from the state was first propounded by Hegel in his book 'Philosophy of Rights'. According to him civil society occupies the space between family and state. The state and civil society depend on each other, yet their relation is full of tensions and requires a complicated balancing act (Anheier and List, 2005). He saw civil society as the successor to the family and predecessor to state.

Civil society is not a homogenous entity, but a space in which citizens organise in promotion of diverse interests and forms of action that will likely be inconsistent with each other. (Cameron,2008). It is a sphere of social interaction between the economy and state, composed of actors and organisations that self-organise to advance collective goals. As this definition suggests, the term 'civil society' refers to the space of collective public action as well as the actors and institutions that populate the space. Efforts to analyse civil society, therefore, have primarily focused on disaggregating the actors and organisations within the public sphere in order to draw conclusions about the 'strength' or 'impact' of different elements of civil society (Cohen and Arato: 1992). From the ancient writings of Cicero to the modern John Locke, civil society has been described as the arena of civic participation that extends the practice of democracy to the grass root. Civil society is an all-encompassing field with groups and associations representing various interests, sections, values in the society.

Meaning and Emergence of Civil Society Organisation (CSO):

Civil society has not only altered the way issues and concerns of various sections of society are perceived but is influencing the approach taken to shape different policies at the global and national level. Civil Society Organisations can be described as organised civil society with both formal and informal units like non-governmental organisations, labour unions, self-help groups, community based organisations, expert groups etc. The site at which society enters into relationship with state can be defined as civil society. It is a public sphere where people can pursue self-defined ends in an associational area of common concern. (Chandhoke, 1995). The Institute for Development Studies (IDS) in its concept paper on civil society and good governance defined civil society as "an intermediate realm situated between state and household, populated by organized groups or associations, which are separate from the state, enjoy some autonomy in relations with the state, and are formed voluntarily by members of society to protect or extend their interests, values or identities". CSOs can be defined as organizations, having a formal structure whose members share some common interest. According to International Monetary Fund (IMF) "civil society organization" refers to the wide range of citizen associations that exists in virtually all member countries to provide benefits, services, or political influence to specific groups within society. CSOs include business forums, faith-based associations, labour unions, local community groups, nongovernmental organizations (NGOs), philanthropic foundations, and think tanks, etc. Branches of government (government agencies and legislators), individual businesses, political parties, and the media are usually excluded. Through their work CSOs not only influence and shape the policies at both global and national levels, but also encourage people and society at large to embrace the norms, standards and principles associated with the concept of democracy, equality and social justice. They are responsible for the rise of alternative perspective on development which engages with society and citizens. Rajesh Tandon (2003), defines civil society as a collection of individual and collective initiatives for the common public good.

In today's contemporary world CSOs are considered to be one of the key players in the national political arena – with the ability to bring out reforms in various government sectors. Traditionally, the state is seen and perceived as the central figure in maintaining law and order, regulating the economy and market, providing relief and infrastructure facilities, to carry out the overall developmental activities. However, the failure of the state to do so is the important contributing factor towards the unprecedented growth of CSOs. They are able to reach and penetrate various levels in the society which unfortunately the state has not been able to do so. The political, economic and administrative limitations on state have resulted in the creation of gaps between the government and the masses. In the present era of globalisation, states are under pressure to follow the diktat of the market economy resulting in the withdrawal of the state from its conventional field of operation resulting in the creation of a vacuum, which is being fulfilled by CSOs today. They provide services to the people as well as to the state as. They have come to play a strategic role in offering political, social, legal and welfare assistance to the society. In the past three decades more and more states have adopted the policies of liberalisation and privatisation resulting in the reduction of the scope and role of government agencies and changed the socioeconomic dynamics in the society. Therefore, the challenge before the CSOs is to have a broad understanding about these changes and frame their objectives according to the emerging scenario at all levels: global, national, regional and local.

Prof. Ramesh Sharan has classified the Civil Society Organizations in India into various categories: (Singh, 2000)

i. Gandhian influenced voluntary groups.
ii. Professional rural development agencies by professionals, by Corporate and by smaller groups
iii. Civil and political rights groups
iv. Missionary organizations Christian Mission, R.K. Mission
v. Student, worker and women's movements related to left and other political parties
vi. Independent social movements of Dalits, adivasis, women, environmentalists.
vii. Movements and groups of minorities (Muslim, Christian, Buddhist etc)
viii. Religious movements; both of spiritual and fundamentalist types.

Institution like the IMF and World Bank have been closely working with CSOs as a response to the demands raised by various groups, especially with regard to economic and social justice. CSOs play a central role in their engagement both at global level and national level, especially with underdeveloped countries. As per World Bank CSOs have also become significant players in global development assistance, with the Organization for Economic Cooperation and Development (OECD) estimating that in 2011, USD 19.3 billion in official development assistance was directed through them. CSOs have also demonstrated an increased influence and ability to shape global public policy during the past two decades. This dynamism is exemplified by successful advocacy campaigns that have mobilized thousands of supporters around the world on issues such as poverty reduction, women empowerment, child rights, governance, economic and social development and climate change. Over the years CSOs have come to play a very important role in humanitarian relief, socio-economic development and improved governance by:

i. Ensuring that voices of poor and marginalized people can be heard by governments, and that their views are factored into policy decisions;
ii. Partnering with governments to provide social services, particularly in fragile governance and post-conflict settings;

iii. Providing technical expertise and offering innovative, participatory, and cost-effective solutions to local problems; and

iv. Strengthening public sector accountability and transparency through increased support for good governance.

IMF and World Bank both engage with CSOs at different stages and levels: like information sharing, policy dialogue, strategy consultation, operational collaboration, and institutional partnerships. According to World Bank CSOs can be classified according to the sector, focus, origins, scale, level of formality, values, or theoretical perspectives. It emphasises that CSOs differ in the degree to which they provide the following five functions:

i representation (organizations that aggregate citizen voice)

ii. technical expertise (organizations that provide information and advice, and lobby on particular issues)

iii. capacity-building (organizations that provide support to other CSOs, including funding)

iv. service-delivery (organizations that implement development projects or provide services)

v. social functions (organizations that foster collective recreational activities)

Traditionally the space for representation of society and people has been occupied by political parties. But over the period time, CSOs have made a foray into this space. CSOs provide an alternative avenue for the various sections in the society to be represented independent of political parties. Giving them an opportunity to raise their issues and concerns without being influenced by political elites, public authority, etc. Alexis de Tocqueville while describing the early 19th century America stated that the civic associations provided a bulwark against majority rule by advancing marginal issues and the diverse causes of minority groups (Mansfield and Winthrop, 2000). CSOs aim to change the prevalent and established rules to integrate and foster the changes in the society.

CSOs can draw attention to various social-economic issues by placing them on the agenda thereby influencing the Government's policy process. As governments and public authorities are seeking legitimacy, try to understand the needs of the population and attempt to fulfil their regulatory and welfare missions in the best possible way, CSOs are the indispensable link between people and public authorities (Desse, 2012). The services provided by the CSOs are either with the cooperation of public authorities or independently. There is no uniformity on the structures and contours of CSOs. They are diverse in terms of their issues, nature, functions, members etc. According to Anil C. Shah there few parameters to access the functionality of CSOs.(Singh, 2012).

i. Level of participation by people
ii. Nature of technical excellence
iii. Cost – effectiveness of operations
iv. Equity
v. Institutional, financial and environmental sustainability
vi. Accountability to the stakeholders.

Influence of Civil Society Organization on Legislative Procedures:

India has a vibrant civil society consisting of a wide range of associations, groups and organisations. Civil Society Organizations (CSOs) play a very vital and crucial role in upholding the democratic values and ethos prevalent in the society. Over the years CSOs have acted as bridges between the government and the public. They provide a platform for the common masses to present their opinions pertaining to matters of public importance. It also gives an opportunity to maintain public accountability of the legislature towards the people. The work done by various CSOs on a multitude of issues confronting the society today provides valuable information and data required to initiate significant legislations directed towards delivering the goals enunciated in the Constitution of India. CSOs are helping the legislature in steering the objective of social goals through the realm of public policy and by initiating major social reforms required to upheld the principle of equality for all. India has more than two million CSOs dedicated to diverse interests ranging from environment to child rights to education to women rights to the protection of civil rights etc. Over the year's they have become the torch-bearers of social reforms in the country. Decentralisation has brought with it autonomy for all the state governments to carve out state/region specific programmes for better implementation of the various policies. (Sayal, 2011).

Civil Society has a long history in India. Social reformers like Raja Ram Mohun Roy, Ishwar Chandra VidyaSagar, Swami Dayanand Saraswati, Jyotiroa Govindrao Phule, Savitribai Phule, Pandita Ramabai have played a leading role in bringing about the social transformation in the country. Brahmo Samaj, Satya Shodhak Samaj, Arya Samaj, Prarthna Samaj are some of the notable organizations who had relentlessly pursued the social reforms in the society during the colonial period. CSOs got ample opportunity to grow during colonial period. The emergence of Indian renaissance in the late 19th century fostered the growth of various civil society movements and organisations. Taking this legacy forward, India after independence especially in the last few decades has witnessed an unprecedented growth in civil society movements and of civil society organisations. The Chipko Movement (1973), Narmada Bachao Andolan (1989 onwards), the Right to Information Movement and others are the social movements which were started by ordinary citizens and have played an important role in empowering the weaker section of the society. CSOs in India are associated with a myriad of issues and subjects like - environment, protection of civil and political right, women's empowerment, protection of child rights, education, governance and accountability, sanitation etc. According to Rajni Kothari (1993) voluntarism has been integral part of the Indian civilisation which is primarily cultural in nature rather than political. Organisations based on caste, religion have been in existence for a long time. He further argues that the real functioning of the state to a very large extent was enabled by these organizations. CSOs are providing supplementary support to the state in its development endeavours.

CSOs today are playing a decisive role in the legislative process by influencing the policy process of the Government. They are recognised as the essential "third sector" working towards strengthening the various aspects of civil society. CSOs are directly involved in the public policy process today, giving valuable inputs, information and relevant data. They are also increasingly being viewed as instruments of transparency, accountability, good governance, effective public service, etc. Indian society consists of various groups and entities putting enormous pressure on the government, demanding their rights and share. The inability of the Indian state to overcome the various challenges which arose due to the increasing demands of the society has encouraged and paved the way for the CSOs. The state no longer solely occupies the traditional space in the context of meeting the aspirations of the people. The emergence of large numbers of CSOs in the last few decades can be attributed as an answer to the failure of state institutions and abuse of power by figures of public authority.

The emergence of large numbers of CSOs in the last few decades can be attributed as an answer to the failure and withdrawal of state institutions. 1990s heralded the era of liberalisation and privatisation in the country. Under the guidance of the World Bank and IMF, India adopted the structural adjustment program with emphasis on enhanced role of private sector and reduction of Government roles especially in the matters related to market and economy. With the gradual decline in scope, functions and responsibility of the Indian state, CSOs emerged as the main course of avenue in promoting non-state activities. With more than 1.25 billion population, the capacity of Indian state is stretched to its limit.It is in this context that CSOs have emerged as front runners in carrying out the functions generally considered to be the state domain. An important point to remember here is that the CSOs must work as per the neoliberal agenda of the state. CSOs play a very important role by disseminating crucial information regarding various developmental policies and schemes of the government and by making people aware of their rights and entitlement. They not only enable the common man to participate in administrative process, but also makes the administration more approachable and people friendly.

In the past few decades the CSOs involvement in policy formulation and implementation has become a major part in the political life across the globe. The legislative procedures and policy making are complex processes requiring a multitude of research, data, and information. The Parliament of India, through legislation meets the demands and aspiration of the society. Various organisations today provide avenues for the common man to access all the information pertaining to the legislative business conduct in both the houses. In a developing country like India, where the responsibility to provide social welfare rests primarily with the state, the public policy process assumes greater significance. Public policy is formulated and implemented through a plethora of formal and informal institutions, mechanism and processes. (Mathur, 2009). The formulation of public policy is a difficult process which involves the interaction of a complex set of forces. It begins with the ideas citizens or civil society organizations have about the actions they want the government to take. (Sapru:2010). The government can ask for the suggestions from CSOs even before the Bill has been drafted. In 2005, the Government of India has asked various CSOs to send in their suggestions for the draft of the New Police Act. The current police act dated back to 1861 during the colonial period. The government felt the need to reform the law as per the new challenges and demand raised over a period of time.

Their programs and plans are directly linked to the policies that are formulated by the government. Their inputs are valuable not only for the proper formulation of legislations but also for the efficient execution on the ground level. The Joint Committee for The Scheduled Tribes (Recognition of Forest Rights) Bill, 2005 received more than 100 suggestions from various organisations working on the subject of environment, land and tribal rights, giving them an opportunity to get involved in the policy making process. CSOs provide the governments with necessary information required to bring the maximum number of people within the ambit of the policy.

CSOs play a very critical role by presenting evidence to the legislative bodies required to make necessary changes in policies. They advocate crucial changes in laws, legislations, rules pertaining to the administration required to meet the demands raised by various groups within the society. Through their work they are making people aware about their rights and entitlement. The success of the public policy today depends to a very large extent on the effective response of the CSOs. Their engagement both with government and society has led to constructive changes in important legislation as they are considered to be substantive contributors in realising the developmental goals pursued by the state. The Government of India often seeks advice and suggestion from CSOs on various issues, bringing together a plethora of ideas on reforms. CSOs are not only involved with the formulation of policy, but they have become imperative for the successful implementation of the policies as well. The Government of India has recognised the vast potential of the CSOs and has been actively engaged with them. In the year 2007, the Planning Commission (presently known as NITI Aayog) brought in the national policy on voluntary sector in India.

The state agencies and institutions often include various CSOs in furthering the development goals pursued by Government of India. For example, the Council for Advancement of People's Action and Rural Technology (CAPART), actively involves various CSOs for the rural development. The 7th Five Year Plan emphasised the importance of the voluntary sector and creation of CAPART in 1986, as the nodal agency for facilitating and harnessing the partnership between the voluntary sector and Government of India towards the development of the rural sector in India. With the introduction of the policy of liberalisation in the early 1990s, the Indian state underwent a huge transformation. The Structural Adjustment Programs (SAP) restructured the entire Indian economy with emphasis on market forces, private actor etc. This paved the way for the non-state actors, especially CSOs to grow and take the lead in providing benefits to the people and enhanced their role in overall policy process. CSOs are part of the entire process from formulation to implementation.

Economic reforms and liberalisation coincided with the process of decentralisation introduced through the 73rd and 74th Constitutional Amendment Act, empowering the village Panchayats and Municipals Corporations respectively considerably compared to the earlier period. It gave greater decision-making power to the local government which in turn increased the scope of the role played by CSOs in various capacities at local level and also people's participation. With the passing of important legislation like Right to Information (2005) and the Community Participation Law (2005) the citizens were further empowered across the spectrum. The Community Participation Bill, also known as the Nagar Raj Bill focussed on the reforms to encourage participation in the decision-making process especially at the lower level in the urban areas.

As a part of the urban reform process this Bill emphasized on the subject of governance with effective engagement with the CSOs as part of the Jawaharlal Nehru National Urban Renewal Mission (JNNURM), which primarily focusses on developing urban infrastructure and services. CSOs play a very important role of watching and checking the implementation of the work undertaken by state governments under this policy. In this regard the Centre for Civil Society (CCS) is the nodal agency for CSOs in Delhi for the implementation of schemes under JNNURM. CSS is a non-profit independent organisation working in the field of decentralisation, policy reforms, sustainable development, education etc. It actively participates in the formulation of developmental plans for Delhi. It coordinates with various organizations for better implementation of plans under JNNURM. The failure of the states to address the economic, social and political demands of the society has not only reduced people's faith in it but has strengthened the position of CSOs. The passing of 73rd and 74th Amendment Act in 1991 ushered a new era of decentralisation in the country. This affected not only the political dynamics at the local level, but also enhanced the scope of engagement with CSOs especially at the level of service delivery due to the constraints on state.

The demand for transparency by CSOs is one of the prerequisites for governance. Access to timely and relevant information became the foundation for the Right to Information Movement (RTI) (Vyasulu,2007). The RTI movement was started by the Mazdoor Kisan Shakti Sangathan (MKSS), an organization located in the Devdungri village of Rajasthan which is a drought prone region in the state. This organization was led by a social activist Aruna Roy. It is an organization of peasants and workers and has successfully demonstrated the power of information as an effective tool to enable citizens to participate in governance. The reverberations of this struggle led to a nationwide demand for a law to guarantee the right to information to every citizen, with widespread support from social activists, professionals, lawyers, and persons within the bureaucracy, politics and the media, who are committed to transparent and accountable governance and people's empowerment (Mander and Joshi: 1999). The Government of Rajasthan had started famine-relief programmes, such as construction of roads and water tanks with the twin objective of providing livelihood to poor daily labourers and develop infrastructure in the area. Rajasthan already had minimum wages act, but the wages paid to the labourers and workers was lower than that even though the official documents mention that the entries made were as per the minimum wages. MKSS demanded the access to the records of expenditures made by Panchayats for the implementation of government schemes on livelihood. It was during their campaign for the payment of minimum wages, started in 1988, that the group realized that unless government accounts and records were made available to people for scrutiny, government officials would continue to deny the payment of minimum wages (Mohanty, 2006). In 1998, the Government of Rajasthan amended the Panchayati Raj Act, giving access to documents pertaining to all the subjects under the purview of Panchayats. The movement started by MKSS was supported by many grass root organizations demanding access and information to government records. The relentless work done by various CSOs led to formulation of RTI at state level in the year 2000. TheNational Campaign for People's Right to Information, a coalition of several CSOs was established in 1996 to press for the creation of RTI at the national level. The RTI was an essential tool in combating the corrupt practices by public institutions and authorities. The Government of Indiaconstituted the H.D. Shourie Committee in 1997 to prepare a draft legislation on freedom of information. However, it was never introduced in Parliament. In 2004, the National Advisory Council (NAC), met with Aruna Roy and several members from the civil society to discuss about the changes in the Freedom of India Act. In December 2004, the RTI Bill was tabled in the Lok Sabha. This Bill was largely based on the recommendations made by the NCPRI. In June 2005, the RTI Bill became an Act which gave every citizen the right to question, examine, audit, review and assess government acts and decision, to ensure that these are consistent with the principles of public interest, probity and justice (Mohanty,2006).

The Ministry of Women and Child Development through the UJJWALA scheme has been working with various CSOs towards the prevention of trafficking, rehabilitation of women and children. The Ministry often engages with the CSOs for consultation and suggestion so that a comprehensive policy could be drafted towards making more stringent laws to provide relief to the victims of trafficking. In 2010, the Ministry held intense discussion with CSOs from the across the county under the UJJWALA scheme to develop an all-inclusive policy to combat the menace of trafficking. CSOs like Beti Foundation, Indian Women Human Welfare Society, Jagriti, Rural Education for Action and Development Agency have been involved in consultation with the Government through this Ministry for creating mechanisms to address the various issues and challenges involved with human trafficking.

In a democratic country like India, the ultimate responsibility for providing the citizens with basic opportunities and facilities rests on the state. With the ever-growing demands from the society along with changing socio-economic dynamics, the role played by CSOs has increased to a large extent. Over the past few decades the Government of India has actively engaged with CSOs at policy level. The policies initiated by the state have been significantly influenced by CSOs. The Food Security Act (2013) is one of the finest examples of how CSOs have influenced Government policies. The credit for this goes to People's Union for Civil Liberties (PUCL). In 2001, PUCL filed a PIL in the Supreme Court of India exposing the amount food grains going waste due to non-availability of proper storage facility in the country and seek legal enforcement of Right to Food. They argued that these food grains could be used to feed the starving population. This also exposed the weak public distribution mechanism in the country. The Supreme Court affirmed the Right to Food as inevitable and upheld Article 21 of the Constitution of India, which guarantees the fundamental right to "life with human dignity." The Food Corporation of India (FCI) was ordered to ensure that food grains do not decay and are distributed wisely. In 2009, the President of India announced the formulation of the National Food Security Act to provide families below poverty line (BPL) with food grains at highly subsidised and nominal rates. Accordingly, in 2013, the National Food Security Act was passed by the Parliament of India. The initiative taken by the PUCL has not only paved the way for an important legislation providing social security for the BPL families, but also highlighted the role played by CSOs in the policy process.

With the growing constraints on the Indian state, CSOs are regarded as the agents of social change in the country. For example, the Anti-

Corruption Movement led by Anna Hazare – a Gandhian Social Activist united the entire country against the widespread corruption prevalent in all the echelons of the society. The movement made it imperative for the Indian Parliament to initiate a strong and robust anti-corruption law – The Lokpal Bill. The Jan Lokpal Bill (People's Ombudsman Bill) was drafted by the members of India Against Corruption notably by N. Santosh Hegde, former Justice of Supreme Court of India and Lokayukta of Karnataka (2006-2011), Prashant Bhushan, Senior Supreme Court Lawyer and Arvind Kejriwal (present Chief Minister of Delhi). This draft called for more stringent laws and power under the purview of Lokpal than was mentioned in draft prepared by the Government of India in 2010. In April 2011, Anna Hazare and other members of India Against Corruption demanded that a joint committee be formed comprising of representatives from both the Union Government and civil society for drafting a stronger Lokpal Bill. During drafting stage, the joint committee was unable to form a consensus regarding the powers and functions of the Lokpal. In July 2011,Union Cabinet approved the draft of the Lokpal Bill amidst criticism from various civil society organizations. After carefully reviewing the provisions of the Bill Anna Hazare rejected the draft stating that the Government of India disregarded the voices of people. The anti-corruption movement led by Anna Hazare gained huge momentum bringing together people from all walks of life thus creating a strong civil society opposition to the Government's draft. The Jan Lokpal Bill was finally passed in 2013. Though the Jan Lokpal Bill passed by the Government doesn't reflect all the provisions enumerated by Anna Hazare but nonetheless it was due to the sheer pressure from the civil society that Parliament finally passed the bill in 2013.

According to the global civil society alliance, CIVICUS, due to the bureaucratic harassment and defamatory statement by government officials about the civil society organisations operating in India have contributed towards a rise of prohibitive operating environment for India's civil society. The civil society plays a crucial role in holding the government accountable for proper and effective implementation of laws and policies. The impact of CSOs on creating pressure on the legislature regarding effective pieces of legislation is huge. Despite playing a positive and constructive role towards the society at large, nevertheless, their strategies and performance have been criticised to a certain extent. In 2014, Intelligence Bureau's report on impact of NGOs on development stated that the organisations which are receiving funds from the foreign countries are serving their interest and stalling the developmental process in India.As a result, the Government of India in 2017, submitted stringent guidelines to the Supreme Court regarding accreditation of CSOs/ NGOs/VOs. These guidelines are meant to regulate the process through which they receive grants, maintaining and auditing of accounts properly.

Conclusion

CSOs have become necessary in the current framework where market forces have come to dominate the relationship between state and society so that the effective and responsive system of governance could be established and maintained. They don't only play a critical role towards providing facilities to the marginalized section, but at the same time they are facilitating interaction between the government and various stakeholders in the society. The gradual increase in the role played by the CSOs has made them an integral part of the policy process in the country. Since the independence, the voluntary sector has come a long way in India. Their growth and transformation has made them indispensable - both for the government and the society. In developing countries like India, where the primary responsibility to carry out the developmental process lies with the state, but due to its limitation the state is unable to do so. This in turn led to the emergence of CSOs, who are helping the state in carrying out its responsibilities effectively. They are transforming the nature of government service delivery mechanism by introducing a timely intervention required to strengthen the implementation process of the policy.

Review Question:

1. Define the concept of Civil Society Organisation.
2. Describe the emergence and significance of Civil Society Organisations in India.
3. Explain the role of Civil Society Organisation as the third tier of the government.

4. What is Right to Information Act?
5. Write a short note on Food Security Bill.

References:

1. Anheier and Regina A. List., (2005). "A Dictionary of civil society, philanthropy and the non-profit sector", Taylor & Francis Ist ed.
2. Cameron, Geoffrey. (2008). "Background paper: How should we classify civil society? A review of mainstream and alternative approaches". International Conference: Whatever Happened to Civil Society? International NGOs Training and Research Centre.
3. Chandhoke, Neera, (1995). "State and Civil Society: Explorations in Political Theory", Sage Publications, New Delhi
4. "Civil Society and Governance' – A Concept Paper". (1999). Institute for Development Studies.
5. Cohen, Jean and Andrew Arato, (1992). "Civil Society and Political Theory" Cambridge: MIT Press.
6. Consultations with civil society organisations. (2000). The International Bank for Reconstruction and Development/The World Bank. http://siteresources worldbank.org/INTRANET SOCIALDEVELOPMENT/873204-1111663470099/ 20489515/ ConsultationsWithCSOsGuidelines.pdf Accessed on 7.3.20
7. Court, Julius, Enrique Mendizabal, David Osborne and John Young, (2006). "Policy Engagement: How Civil Society Can be More Effective. Overseas Development Institute". https://www.odi.org/publications/160-policy-engagement-how-civil- society-can-be-more-effective
8. Government of India, (2007). ""National Policy on Voluntary Sector", Voluntary Action Cell, Planning Commission, Government of India. http://planningcommission.gov.in/data/ngo/npvol07.pdf. Accessed on 23.03.2017
9. Hudson, Alex, (2006). "CSOs and Parliamentary Committees The UK's International Development Select Committee". Overseas Development Institute, UK. https://www.odi.org/sites/odi.org.uk/files/ odi-assets/ events- documents/2918.pdf Accessed on 24.12.2016

10. Manor, James, Mark Robinson and Gordon White (1999). "Civil Society and Governance" – A Concept Paper. Institute of Development Studies, University of Sussex, England. http://cide.oise.utoronto.ca/civil_society/resources/Manor%20Robinson%20and% 20White%20Concept%20 Paper.pdf Accessed on 19.10. 2017

11. Mansfield, Harvey and Delba Winthrop, (2000). "Democracy in America. Alexis de Tocqueville", University of Chicago Press. (Ed.)

12. Mathur, Kuldeep, (2009) "From Government to Governance: A Brief Survey of the Indian Experience", NBT, New Delhi

13. Mander, Harsh & Abha Joshi, (1999). "The Movement for Right to Information in India", Commonwealth Human Rights Initiative. http://www.humanrightsinitiative.org. Accessed on 9.06.2017

14. Mohanty, Bijaya Kumar,(2005). "The Growing role of Civil Society Organisations in Contemporary India: A Case Study of the Mazdoor Kisan Shakti Sangathan". Centre for Studies in Social Sciences, Calcutta.

15. Sapru, RK, (2010), "Public Policy: Art and Craft of Policy Analysis", PHI, New Delhi.

16. Sayal, Reetika, (2011) "Civil Society Organisaiona and Elementary Education in Madhya Pradesh". The Institute for Social and Economic Change

17. Singh, Vijender, (2012). "An Analysis of Concept and Role of Civil Society in Contemporary India", Global Journal of Human Social Science Volume 12 Issue 7

18. Scholte, Jan Aart, (2001). "Civil Society and Democracy in Global Governance", CSGR Working Paper No. 65/01. Centre for the Study of Globalisation and Regionalisation (CSGR), University of Warwick.

19. "The Future Role of Civil Society", (2013). World Scenario Series. World Economic Forum

20. Tandon, R., (2003). "The Civil Society – Governance Interface", In R. Tandon & R. Mohanty (Ed.) "Does Civil Society Matters: Governance in Contemporary India", Sage Publications

21. United Nations, (2005). "A Guide to Civil Society Organisations working on Democratic Governance", United Nations Development Programme,

Bureau for Development Policy, Democratic Governance Group, New York http://www.undp.org/content/dam/aplaws/publication/en/publications/democratic-governance/oslo-governance-center/civic-engagement/a-guide-to-civil-society-organizations-working-on-democratic-governance-/3665%20Booklet_heleWEB_.pdf Accessed on 10.01.2017

ANNEXURE

Lok Sabha

Sl. No.	Name of the Committee	Whether elected or nominated	No. of members	Term
1.	Business Advisory Committee	Nominated	15	Till reconstituted
2.	Committee on Private Members' Bills and Resolutions	Nominated	15	One year
3.	Committee on Petitions	Nominated	15	Till reconstituted
4.	Committee on Estimates	Elected	30	One year
5.	Committee of Privileges	Nominated	15	Till reconstituted
6.	Committee on Subordinate Legislation	Nominated	15	One year
7.	Committee on Government Assurances	Nominated	15	One year
8.	Committee on Absence of Members from the Sittings of the House	Nominated	15	One year

9.	Rules Committee	Nominated	15	Till reconstituted
10.	General Purposes Committee	Nominated	@	Till reconstituted
11.	House Committee	Nominated	15	One year
12.	Public Accounts Committee	Elected	22 (15-Lok Sabha) (7-Rajya Sabha)*	One year
13.	Committee on Public Undertakings	Elected	22 (15- Lok Sabha) (7-Rajya Sabha)*	One year
14.	Library Committee	Nominated	9 (6- Lok Sabha) (3-Rajya Sabha)*	One year
15.	Committee on the Welfare of Scheduled Castes and Scheduled Tribes	Elected	30 (20-Lok Sabha) (10-Rajya Sabha)*	One year
16.	Committee on Papers Laid on the Table	Nominated	15	One year

@ Consisting of the Speaker, the Deputy Speaker, members of the Panel of Chairmen, Chairmen of all Standing Committees of the Lok Sabha, leaders of recognized parties and groups and such other members as may be nominated by the Speaker.

* Members of the Rajya Sabha are also associated with these Committees.

Rajya Sabha

Sl. No.	Name of the Committee	Whether elected or nominated	No. of members	Term
1.	Business Advisory Committee	Nominated	11 (including Chairman & Deputy Chairman)	Till recon-stituted
2.	Committee of Privileges	Nominated	10	-do-
3.	Committee on Petitions	Nominated	10	-do-
4.	Committee on Rules	Nominated	16	-do-
5.	Committee on Subordinate Legislation	Nominated	15	-do-
6.	Committee on Government Assurances	Nominated	10	-do-
7.	House Committee	Nominated	7	-do-
8.	General Purposes Committee	Nominated	@@	*
9.	Committee on Papers Laid on the Table	Nominated	10	Till recon-stituted
10.	Committee on MPLAD Scheme	Nominated	10	Tenure of the Members (in RS)
11.	Ethics Committee	Nominated	10	Till recon-stituted
12.	Committee on Provision of Computers to MPs (RS)	Nominated	7	Tenure of the Members (in RS)

@@ Consisting of the Chairman, Deputy Chairman, panel of Vice Chairman, Chairman of all Standing Committees of the Rajya Sabha, Leaders of recognized parties and groups and such other members as may be nominated by the Chairman.

* Not provided in the rules but is constituted every year.

Committees

Sl. No.	Name of the Committee	Whether elected or nominated	No. of members	Term
1.	Joint Committee on Salaries and Allowances of Members of Parliament	Nominated	15 (10- Lok Sabha) (5-Rajya Sabha)	One year
2.	Joint Committee on Offices of Profit	Elected	15 (10- Lok Sabha) (5-Rajya Sabha)	Co-terminus with the life of Lok Sabha
3.	Committee on the Empowerment of Women	Nominated	30 (20-Lok Sabha) (10-Rajya Sabha)	One year
4.	Joint Parliamentary Committee on the Functioning of Wakf Boards	Nominated	30 (20-Lok Sabha) (10-Rajya Sabha)	No fixed tenure
5.	Joint Committee on Security in Parliament House Complex	Nominated	10 (7-Lok Sabha) (3- Rajya Sabha)	No fixed tenure

Source: http://www.mpa.nic.in/mpa/Manual/Manual_English/Annexure/annex-23.htm

Standing Committees	
Financial Committees (Committee on Estimates, Public Undertakings, and Public Accounts)	Exclusively under the Lok Sabha secretariat. A Minister is not eligible to be a member. • Estimates Committee examines estimates of ministries. Public Undertakings Committee (PUC) examines functioning of public undertakings and Public Accounts Committee (PAC) scrutinises the statement of accounts showing the sums granted by Parliament for the expenditure of the government.
	• Customarily, chairperson of PAC is an Opposition member. PAC can hear non-official witnesses.
	• Estimates Committee elects 30 members only from the Lok Sabha. The Committees on Public Accounts and Public Undertakings have 7 Rajya Sabha members out of a total of 22 members.
Departmentally Related Standing Committees (Committees on Agriculture, Commerce, Home Affairs, Health and Family Welfare, etc.)	• Departmentally Related Standing Committees (DRSCs) were introduced in 1993 to ensure oversight over each ministry. A Minister is not eligible to be a member. • May hear expert witnesses and representatives of special interest groups. • There are 24 DRSCs. Committees such as Home Affairs, Finance and External Affairs are customarily chaired by a member of opposition party. • Each DRSC has 31 members, with 21 from Lok Sabha and 10 from Rajya Sabha. Seats on each Committee are allocated to parties in proportion to their strength in the House. The Chairs of the Committee are appointed by the Speaker or Chairman of each House.

Other Standing Committees (Business Advisory Committee, Committee on Petitions, Subordinate Legislations, and Government Assurances, Joint Committees on Salaries and Allowances of MPs and Office of Profit)	• Each House has a set of these Committees, to inquire into other matters related to Parliament and the day-to-day business of the House. Lok Sabha has 16 Committees and Rajya Sabha has 12. Rajya Sabha classifies Committees on Ethics, MPLADs, and Provision of Computers to Members of RS as Standing Committees. • Number of members varies between 7 and 26. Some have fixed term of one year while others have no fixed term. A Minister is not eligible to be a member of the Committees on Women Empowerment; Government Assurances; Petitions; Subordinate Legislation; and Welfare of SC/STs. • Joint Committees include members (elected or nominated) from both Houses. Such Committees have about 15 members and are formed for a term of one Lok Sabha.
Adhoc Committees	

Committees on Ethics, MPLADS, and Provision of Computers to LS Members, Joint Committees on Wakf, Railway Convention, Fertiliser Pricing, etc.

- Appointed for a specific purpose, such as the Joint Committee to examine pricing of telecom licenses and spectrum. They cease to exist after the task assigned to them is over. Lok Sabha classifies Committees on Ethics, MPLADS & Computers as Ad Hoc Committees.
- Include Select and Joint Committees on Bills, e.g., Commercial Division of High Courts Bill, 2009.
- Except for the Joint Committee on Wakf, the Committees operate in the Lok Sabha. Include members from both Houses and the number varies between 10 and 30.

Sources: "Parliamentary Committees Introduction," Lok Sabha website and "Committees of Rajya Sabha," Rajya Sabha website; PRS

Appointed for a specific purpose, such as the Joint Committee to examine pricing of telecom licenses and spectrum. They cease to exist after the task assigned to them is over. Lok Sabha classifies Committees on Ethics, MPLADS & Computers as Ad Hoc Committees.

- Include Select and Joint Committees on Bills, e.g., Commercial Division of High Courts Bill, 2009.
- Except for the Joint Committee on Wakf, the Committees operate in the Lok Sabha. Include members from both Houses and the number varies between 10 and 30.

Sources: "Parliamentary Committees Introduction," Lok Sabha website and "Committees of Rajya Sabha," Rajya Sabha website; PRS

Index

73rd amendment, 49-50
74th amendment, 13, 59, 66-67, 161

Appropriation Act, 125, 134

Bill, 70-84, 87-91
Budget, 95, 104-05

Calling Attention Motion, 32-33
Civic Culture, 2
Civil Society Organisations 151-52, 157, 164-67
Civil Society, 151-53, 156-57, 159, 161-62, 164-67
Consolidated fund of India, 124-26, 133
Constitution, 69-72, 75-78, 80-83, 86-87, 89-91
Contingency Fund of India, 125-26
Cut Motions 130, 132

Defection, 29
Delegated Legislation 106, 113
Demands for grants, 104-06
Democracy. 139, 143-46, 149-50
Direct Democracy, 3, 4, 6

Electoral College, 26, 39
Exechequer, 116
Executive, 5-7, 9-10, 12, 17-20, 23

Federalism 11
Finance Bill, 126, 128, 131, 133-34
Food Security, 163, 166

Gender Budget, 123
Globalisation, 2, 153, 167
Governance, 1-2, 13-14, 18, 22, 24
Gram sabha, 46, 49-50, 53-54, 67
Green Budget, 124,

International Monetary Fund, 152

Judiciary, 10

Legislative Process, 1, 15, 20, 21, 23
Legislature, 5-7, 10-20, 22-23, 69-70, 72, 81, 83-86, 89-91,
Liberalisation, 153, 158, 160
Line-Item Budget, 120-21
Lok Sabha television, 147

Lok sabha, 69, 71-72, 74-80, 82-85, 87, 90-91
Lokpal, 164

Media, 138-150
Money Bill, 133-34
MPLADS 34, 35, 40
Municipal corporation, 58-59, 64-66

Newspapers, 138-40, 142, 149
NITI Aayog, 160
No-Confidence Motion, 32-33

Panchayat, 42-62, 66-68
Parliament, 69-73, 76-91
Parliamentary Committees, 32,
Parliamentary democracy, 4, 6, 9, 11, 17, 23,
Parliamentary system. 69-70
Parliamentary-committee, 94, 96-97, 99-01, 107-09, 114-15
Performance Budget, 121-22,
President, 69, 71-72, 74-77, 79-83
Private member bill, 71, 76-78, 90-91
Public Accounts, 126

Question Hour, 32-33, 39
Quorum, 102

Rajya sabha, 69, 71-72, 75, 77, 79-80, 83-85, 87, 89, 92
Representative Democracy, 3, 5, 16, 23
Right to Information, 143, 146, 149, 157, 160-62, 166-67

Social media, 142-43, 149
Standing committee. 73, 86-90, 94, 97-98, 100-01, 103, 110-15
State, 151-53, 155, 157-66
Subordinate legislation, 84-86, 90-91

UJJWALA, 162-63

Westminster Model, 93
World Bank,, 154-55, 158, 166

Zero Based Budget, 122-23
Zero Hour, 32-33

About the Authors

Dr. Moitri Dey is currently working as Assistant Professor in the Department of Political Science, Mata Sundri College for Women, Delhi University. She has done her Ph.D in Political Science from the Department of Political Science, Jamia Millia Islamia. She has also published a book entitled "MGNREGA: Success or Failure!", various research papers, chapters in books and articles in reputed journals.

Ms. Paromita Datta is currently teaching as Assistant Professor in the Department of Political Science, Mata Sundri College for Women, University of Delhi. She has done her M.Phil from Centre for Political Studies, Jawaharlal Nehru University and is currently pursuing her Ph.D. from the same. Her areas of interest are state politics, federalism.

Dr. Radha Kumari is currently working as Assistant Professor in the Department of Political Science, Mata Sundri College, Delhi University. She has done her Ph.D. in Gandhian Peace Studies from University of Rajasthan, Jaipur. She has also published articles and chapters in research journals and text books.

Dr. Simer Preet Kaur is currently working as Assistant Professor in the Department of Political Science, Mata Sundri College for Women, Delhi University. She has done her Ph.D in Political Science from Punjabi University. She has written a book titled 'Indian Parliamentary Democracy in Coalition Era', presented papers in national and international seminars and has published many articles in reputed journals. Her areas of specialization are Indian Government and politics, comparative politics, and constitutional studies.